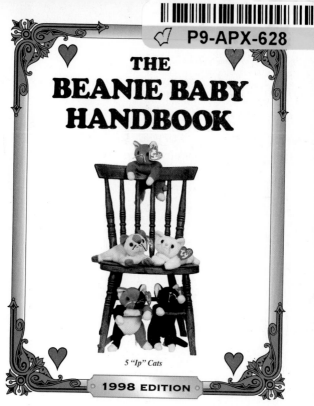

THE
BEANIE BABY
HANDBOOK

5 "Ip" Cats

1998 EDITION

By Les & Sue Fox

SCHOLASTIC INC.
New York Toronto London Auckland Sydney

AN "UNOFFICIAL" HANDBOOK

ISBN 0-439-04168-6

12 11 10 9 8 7 6 5 4 3   8 9/9 0 1 2 3/0

Printed in the U.S.A.   08

First Scholastic printing, September 1998

Beanie Babies™ Are Here To Stay!

Forbes, C. 1996, Jeff Sciortino

H. Ty Warner, Ty, Inc., creator of Beanie Babies

"The Ty Company has caught lightning in a bottle."
– **J. Max Robins, TV Guide**

"Your kids have to have this. Today!"
– **Time Magazine**

"Beanie Babies or bust!"
– **Lauren Kellachan, Playthings Magazine**

"This five-dollar stuffed toy is now in the same league as some of the finest artistic works being created today."
– **Fred Gage, Collectors Jubilee**
(Statement made when Beanie Babies won "Collector's Choice Award" at this major collectibles show.)

"Beanie Babies Are Here To Stay!" is the theme song of Les and Sue Fox's "Unofficial" Beanie Baby Music CD. Ask for it at your favorite store! (See page 207 for lyrics.)

Acknowledgments

The authors of
The Beanie Baby Handbook
wish to express their sincere thanks to:

Joan Verdon
Maggie's Toy Box
Diana Links
Jeanette Long
LaGrange, IL Library
Mark Schaffer
Guy McDaniel

Peggy Gallagher
Holly Hahn
Gina Scaletta
K.C. Walsh
Pam & Bob Brandes
Marc Wolf
Antiques & More

Photos page 17 by Kathleen Duxbury Yeaw

Professional Photography By
Trish Elliott (See son James, page 33)
(Unless otherwise credited)

Book Design By
James J. Ticchio

Games & Puzzles By
Sharon Ticchio

"Find The Hidden Beanies" By
Gerald Bauman

Kids from page 5 (+ Lance the Dog)

Max Chazen
Sam Chazen
Jamie Fox

Carli Franco
Alexandra Long
Hallie Steinfeld

Phoebe Steinfeld
James R. Ticchio
Jessica Ticchio

*Drawing by
Danielle Tucceri,
Boca Raton,
Florida*

Hi, Beanie Kids!

...and Beanie Moms & Dads, Too!

Kid Beanie™

Table of Contents

Professor Beanie's "Fairly Difficult" Beanie Baby Quiz

Professor Beanie™

(Answers on page 214)

1. Which two completely different Beanie Babies share the same poem and birthday?

2. Identify the 10 Beanies with knotted tails.

3. Which *non-Beanie Baby* Ty toys wear official "Beanie Baby Collection" heart tags?

4. Name the 6 blue-eyed Beanie Babies.

5. Do you know which 22 Beanie Babies are predominantly black (or black-striped?)

6. Nineteen Beanies have no legs. Which ones?

7. What color ribbon does Spooky wear? (No peeking.)

8. Name the rabbit *without* a neck ribbon.

9. Only one Beanie Baby comes with two hearts. Who?

10. Only one Beanie Baby shows all his teeth. Who?

11. Who weighs more? Bongo or Congo?

12. After Slither and Hissy, which Beanie Baby has the longest tail?

If you were able to answer all 12 questions correctly (without cheating), **go eat a chili dog!**

Help Beanie Bandito Find His Inch The Worm

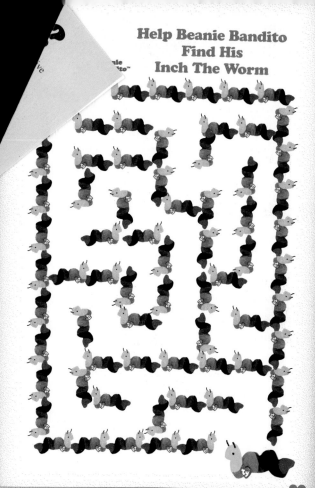

Who am eye?

Can you guess who belongs to each pair of eyes below? We'll g
you a hint – they are all Beanie Babies! (Fill in names on lines.)

1 _____

2 _____

3 _____

4 _____

5 _____

6 _____

7 _____

8 _____

9 _____

10 _____

11 _____

12 _____

(Answers on page 214)

A PERSONAL MESSAGE FROM THE AUTHORS

When Sue and I got married in 1968 (September 2nd marks our 30th anniversary), I made her a promise. "We may never be rich," I told her, "but our life will be filled with surprises."

That promise has definitely been kept. And among all the many surprises in our life, none has been more "unbelievable" than The Beanie Baby Handbook. Over 1 million copies of last year's handbook were sold in more than 10,000 stores across the country. In October, 1997, our cute little 128 page collector's guide actually hit #8 on The New York Times bestseller list! (We also made it to #25 in U.S.A. Today.)

To be honest, I always expected to write a bestseller. However, I was convinced it would be a novel. In 1995, Sue and I collaborated on the fictitious story of "the secret son of Elvis." No one would publish it, so *we* did. The novel was titled "Return To Sender." All of our friends thought it was great. In fact, even the Washington Post gave it a decent review. We printed 5,000 copies, sold 200 and lost $60,000. What an embarrassment when we threw an Elvis birthday party on January 8, 1996 at a Border's superstore in Fort Lauderdale. Hundreds of Elvis fans showed up for free cake and an Elvis impersonator. Not one partygoer bought our book. We were crushed.

Back to the drawing board. After all, John Grisham's first novel wasn't a big success either. (It sold only 7,500 copies.) Determined to take America by storm, Sue and I penned a 500-page Presidential assassination thriller. The movie version would star Liam Neeson as a Secret Service Agent and Michelle Pfeiffer as a political activist. With some persistence, we landed a literary agent who loved the book. Unfortunately, a dozen top publishers didn't. The manuscript is in our garage. Six months down the tubes. That was one surprise we could have lived without.

Oh well, Jonathan Kellerman didn't get published until his eighth book, right? Next novel: The bizarre tale of a Connecticut housewife who cracks up when her husband runs off with the kids. What an incredible story. Mother decides to save the American family, but in her demented state justifies murder! Rave reviews from our loyal friends. Our agent hated it so much he dropped us as clients. No one else was interested. Another six months up in smoke. Life goes on.

"Only four more years of writing novels," I promised Sue. "If we don't make it by the millennium, I'm giving up." Sue and I, who work together from our home, launched into our next masterpiece: The saga of a wealthy Irish American family of professional gamblers who make a crazy deal with Bill Gates. We drafted the outline, named the main characters and began casting the movie. (We also drafted a hilarious screenplay titled "No Brainer!" starring Woody Allen and Arnold Schwarzenegger, a gory werewolf story, and an illustrated children's story book called "The Emperor Of Ice Cream" which we hope to publish this spring.)

Fortunately, something stopped us before we failed again. That something, of course, was Beanie Babies. In between writing, Sue and I are actually devoted parents to our wonderful 7 year-old daughter, Jamie. (Jamie's a writer, too. She wrote a great song called "Mom And Dad Stay Together.") So, in addition to roller skating on Saturdays, gymnastics on Tuesdays, drama class on Wednesdays (with actor Wil Horneff), Brownies, Sunday School and a dozen play dates, Sue and I got involved with Jamie's first real hobby, collecting Beanie Babies. Coincidentally, her first Beanie was Ally, who shares a March 14th birthday with her daddy. Jamie's birthday is March 7th, Sue's is February 5th.

It was not an easy decision to go ahead with The Beanie Baby Handbook. Once again, the big publishers turned us down. (Later, we sold Scholastic the rights to a back-to-school "Pocket Edition.") There was no time to waste. Instead of six months, we had only *three weeks* to complete our Beanie Baby collection, photograph it, and write a book that would beat the competition! And dare we risk another chunk of Jamie's college fund on a risky proposition? Yes. We dared.

Welcome to the 1998 edition of The Beanie Baby Handbook. It's a family affair. We love it, and apparently it loves us back. The sun is shining, and we're surrounded by the most adorable baby animals the world has ever seen!

We've found our niche in the world of publishing.

LES, SUE AND JAMIE FOX
WYCKOFF, NEW JERSEY

BEANIE BABY BULLETIN #1

Curly Visits The President!

POLITICALLY CORRECT BEANIES. While attending the Presidential Inauguration on January 23, 1997, third grade teacher Gina Scaletta introduced Beanie companion Curly, to a couple of guys she met. Anyone recognize Bill Clinton and Al Gore? They're the ones without fur!

Copyright 1997 / Gina Scaletta

 11

BEANIE BABY BULLETIN #2

"A Bear For The Princess"

In December, 1997, Ty, Inc. began taking orders for what has proven to be the most exciting Beanie Baby issued to date: A teddy bear named "Princess." Dedicated to Princess Diana, all of Ty's profits from the sale of this toy by Ty, Inc. will be donated to the Princess' favorite charities.

We join Ty in honoring the memory of Diana with this song.

A Bear For The Princess

Copyright 1997 By Les & Sue Fox

You're only a child for a moment,
And life's just a moment in time.
A king or a queen, whatever we've been,
We're only a verse in the rhyme.

The world must always remember
A flower that wilted in Fall.
She misunderstood evil for good
While wishing the best for us all.

Her life flickered less than a moment,
A moment proudly worn.
And left to care, a sweet teddy bear
With a rose and a heart to mourn.

Dance, dance, dance for the Princess,
Oh deep purple bear with a rose on your chest.
Dance, dance, dance for the Princess
So we will never forget.

Two children with hope for the future.
Two lives changed forever one night.
The torch they will carry, perhaps each will marry
A Princess who's filled with delight.

Tomorrow belongs to the children,
With toys and with millions of smiles,
To light up their days, to keep them amazed,
With teddy bears, wishes, with turtles and fishes,
With a purple bandana, to remember Diana,
With a rose and a heart to mourn.

Dance, dance, dance for the Princess
Oh deep purple bear with a rose on your chest.
Dance, dance, dance for the Princess,
So we will never forget.

BEANIE BABY BULLETIN #3

Cubbie Takes the Field!

"Beanie Baby Days" with the Chicago Cubs

Sunday – May 18, 1997

On Opening Day at Wrigley Field (sponsored by Pepsi), guess who was on hand to throw out the first ball? You guessed it! Ty Warner, the Beanie Baby King of America!

Also on hand were 10,000 kids squealing with delight. Why? Because each kid received a free Cubbie and a special commemorative card (currently worth $100) at the Cubs-Giant game.

In addition to the kids, some 30,000 adults filled the stadium to capacity after waiting on line for hours to purchase a ticket.

Saturday – September 6, 1997

Cubbie does it again! On "Back To School Day," another 10,000 kids were given a free Cubbie and a second commemorative card (currently worth $50) at the Cubs-Mets game. During the seventh inning stretch (see next page) the crowd sang along with "Take Me Out To The Ballgame" and kids stood up to shake their Beanies.

We hear Ty and the Chicago Cubs are going to offer more Beanie Baby Days in 1998 and it is rumored that this fun event may be repeated by other major league stadiums around the country. On January 17, 1998, the Philadelphia Eagles kicked off their playoff game with a "Baldy the Eagle" Beanie Baby Day.

"It was a beautiful day at Wrigley Field. The seats were packed. The game was real."*

Photos by
Mary
Kurowski

As shown in these on-the-scene photos, Beanie Babies Days were a big success in Chicago. If you have a magnifying glass (or maybe a microscope), carefully examine the crowded scene. Hidden among that colorful mass of humanity, including Dawn Rhinerson and Rebecca Huss, are thousands of Cubbies!

(*Lyrics from "Cubbie's First Home Run," an unofficial Beanie Baby song)

BEANIE BABY BULLETIN #4

"Unofficial"

BEANIE BABY SONGS MAKE DEBUT!

Sung by "The Beanie Kids" and arranged by a Grammy-winning New York music producer, America's number one family hobby can now be celebrated with lively music.

Written by Les and Sue Fox, these totally original songs include:

★ BEANIE BABIES ARE HERE TO STAY* (Broadway Sound)
★ SPOT WITHOUT A SPOT* (Blues)
★ BONGO AND CONGO* (Jungle Beat/Rap)
★ MEET THE BEANIES* (Alphabet Marching Song)
★ I NEVER MET A BEANIE BABY I DIDN'T LIKE*
    (1950's Rock)
★ BLACKIE THE ICE CREAM BEAR (Folk)
★ LOST AND FOUND (Country & Western)
★ CUBBIE'S FIRST HOME RUN
    (Pop Song Commemorating Wrigley Field)
★ THE BEANIE BABY DINOSAUR STOMP
    (Chomp! Chomp! Chomp! Chomp!)
★ DON'T ASK HIM WHY (His Name is Ty)

*First 5 songs included on Volume 1

You've Never Heard Anything Like This Before!

Ask for our Beanie Baby Music CD (Volume 1) at stores everywhere!
(Lyrics to songs on page 207)

BEANIE BABY BULLETIN #5

Beanie Baby Extravaganza Weekend!
(October 4-5, 1997)

Jamie Fox draws winning entry for Humphrey at the Rowe-Manse Emporium (Clifton, NJ). Some 10,000 kids entered this free raffle.

"Corkey the Clown" and his sidekick, Daisey, were at all 4 stores to entertain kids with magic, mirth and free balloons. (Carmen Maggio, owner of Rowe-Manse Emporium, pretends to be Sparky!)

At New Jersey's largest Beanie Baby showroom, life-size figures of Garcia and Chops beckon shoppers to spend the day in Rowe-Manse Emporium's 50,000 square foot department store extraordinaire.

Joshua Szporn (with twin sister, Rachael) of Montville, New Jersey was the first of 4 kids under 13 years old to win a free Humphrey the Camel at the Foxes' booksigning/charity event.

Les and Sue Fox sign books (and free posters) to raise $2,000 for St. Jude's Children's Hospital.

At Noodle Kidoodle (in Paramus, New Jersey) lines of Beanie Baby lovers waited to meet the authors of "The Beanie Baby Handbook." The Foxes brought along the "10 Rarest Beanies" from their personal collection. (Note: Pouch isn't rare. He was another free giveaway.)

BEANIE BABY BULLETIN #6

"Special Olympics" Maple Bear Pays Tribute To Our Canadian Friends!

Ty Canada (a division of Ty, Inc.) has helped to raise funds for the Sports Celebrities Festival, the fundraising arm of the Canadian Special Olympics.

A large number of Maple Bears (the exclusive, hard-to-find Canadian counterpart to Libearty) have been sold and auctioned in Canada, including the Canadian National Exposition in Toronto last August and TSN cable television network on December 3, 1997.

We praise the Ty company for its interest in social causes and hope that they will also consider supporting endangered species of animals. We also look forward to more Canadian exclusives. (See also: "Maple" and "Britannia" pages in Current Beanies section.)

Note: All prices in this edition of "The Beanie Baby Handbook" are expressed in U.S. Dollars. Values must be converted to Canadian Dollars, English Sterling, German Marks, to reflect proper prices in other countries.

BEANIE BABIES
THE NEVERENDING STORY

Since writing the first edition of The Beanie Baby Handbook (which seems like a lifetime ago), much has happened. Thirty-one new Beanie Babies have been released and twenty-eight have been retired. Last year we predicted that 43 toys would be retired in 1997 and 1998. Not a bad track record.

These exciting changes have dramatically expanded the size of the Beanie Baby collection. A complete set of Beanies now includes 181 different styles. This "body count" covers all discontinued colors and styles, plus the McDonald's Teenie Beanies. And we still have all of them. To be honest, we actually did not have all of the Beanie Babies last year. For example, we only owned four of the twelve Old Face and New Face teddies. This year, our complete set of 12 is pictured as six pairs of the six matching colors. Nor did we own Derby The Horse in his fine yarn mane and tail. These missing toys were acquired from our favorite retired Beanie dealer, Maggie's Toy Box of Des Plaines, Illinois. Kathy Anderson and her daughter, Maureen, have helped us to keep up with the Joneses.

It is said that the value of a "perfect" collection of Beanie Babies (unsoiled fabric, crisp cardboard hang tags) is now more than $40,000. This is probably true, as the days of finding bargain-priced rarities are pretty much history. However, the true thrill of collecting Beanie Babies has little to do with Peanut The Dark Blue Elephant ($2,500), Quackers Without Wings ($1,500) or even Spot Without A Spot ($1,500.) While the longevity of this hobby may be affected by the rare retired Beanies, the beauty of Beanie Baby collecting is that there are always great toys available at only $5 to $7.

A quick glance through this book, or a trip to your favorite Beanie Baby store, will convince you of two things. First, that every toy in the collection is magnificent. And second, that there are literally dozens of affordable Beanies to bring home for yourself, or for your children. With more to come several times a year! In other words, even if you missed out on the early treasures, you will still get your chance to own lots and lots of equally great new Beanie Babies without taking out a second mortgage!

Unfortunately, the demand for every new Beanie Baby is so strong that many of the recent new releases are scarce at the "official" issue price. In fact, tens of thousands of collectors are convinced that some of these toys will be retired before they can buy them at a reasonable price. Thus, we may continue to see this kind of over-reaction drive up the prices of new toys, at least temporarily.

Hopefully, it will only be a matter of time before you obtain your Gobbles the Turkey, or your Batty the Bat without having to lay out $25 apiece. On the other hand, millions of kids never did get their $5 Garcia, and are still in search of their $5 Peace the Bear. All of this mystery gives an added adrenaline rush to the insatiable quest for Beanie Babies. In the end, all of us (except Ty Warner) must sit back and wait for the smoke to clear, and for the toys we want to magically appear on our local store shelves.

The "Secondary" Market

A two-tier Beanie Baby collector's market has developed in response to the lack of availability of specific Beanies. For most of America, Beanie Babies are something to buy at a neighborhood toy, gift, card or flower shop. Here's how it works. Every time you're shopping near a Beanie Baby store, you check out the front door and window. All too often, you will see this familiar sign: "Sorry. No Beanie Babies." Occasionally, your eyes will be greeted by the words you have been waiting to see: "We Have Beanie Babies." All right! The next step is easy. You simply rush into the store, shove everyone out of your way, and grab everything in sight. (Just kidding! This kind of behavior is one of the sad aspects of the hobby.) The correct response is to politely wait your turn in line to make your selections.

However, for the more advanced or impatient collector this whole approach is too slow and incomplete. Nine times out of ten even when "new" Beanie Babies arrive, they're still the same old Beanies, the ones you already have. (Is there anyone in America who *doesn't* own Inch the Worm, or Pinchers the Lobster?) You may be surprised at how scarce some of these toys will be in ten years, but right now you have a craving for Batty the Bat and Blizzard the White Tiger.

So what do you do? The answer for many people is to turn to the Internet, or to the pages of the many collector magazines which now feature articles and advertisements on America's bestselling toy. Gotta have that adorable little Blizzard critter? Well, Amalgamated Beanie Traders in Wichita, Kansas will be happy to supply it...for only $18. Or maybe you'd rather bid on it in an Internet auction. Or perhaps you'd like to E-Mail your "trade offer" to some enterprising fourth grader. In case you think we're kidding about who's online these days, check this out. 9-1/2 year-old "Sara" of Pennsylvania operates her own Web Page (lisa@mailgate. microe.com.) Sara not only sells Beanies, but also holds contests, lists other "good traders'" web sites and spreads such rumors as Mel Gibson may be suing Ty. If you're interested in a terrific primer on Beanies on the Internet, locate a copy of Janie Daniels' recent book, "The Beanie Invasion." This 170-page illustrated reference (retail $13.95) offers an unorthodox look at the Beanie Baby market. Topics include a survey of kids' opinions, discussions with top Beanie dealers and interviews with the most popular Web Sites. Here are the best Beanie Web Sites to log on to: Ty.com, Beanie Mom, the Beanie Babies Buddies Club, Kim 'n Kevin's Collectibles and Lemon Lainey's Beanies. (Ty.com is the Web Site of Ty, Inc. where 10 million rumors evolve into a few "Official Announcements" each time new Beanies are released or retired.)

Beanie Sociology

It hasn't happened yet, but don't be surprised to see someone offering a college course on the social impact of Beanie Babies! Why not? After all, Beanies are found in a majority of American households. Many mothers even organize social events around Beanies (behavior rewards, birthday gifts, planned outings.) In fact, Beanies have begun to replace Tupperware as the topic of conversation among mothers of 3 to 6 year olds. (Note: Tupperware is the perfect vacuum in which to store Beanies.) Conclusion: Beanie Babies may become a permanent fixture in the American social landscape, not to mention a worldwide obsession among both kids and grown-ups.

Bigger Than Barbies

The Nickelodeon cable channel has become must-watch TV for the elementary school crowd. (*Rugrats* and *Doug* are the top-rated shows.) You can't watch "Nick For Kids" without being deluged by commercials for Barbie Dolls. The 15-to-60 second ads are expensive, they're elaborate (sometimes "Disney quality") and they're relentless. Anyone who sits through two hours of Nick is automatically brainwashed with a subconscious desire to run out and buy a dozen Barbies wearing every imaginable hairstyle and fashion outfit.

Yet, despite the fact that Beanie Babies have never been advertised on television (except by McDonalds in April, 1997), Ty's baby animal toys are actually out-selling Barbie, according to reliable sources. *Playthings* magazine lists Beanie Babies at the top of its monthly list of "Mainstay" bestsellers. Which is why we still answer the common question - "How long can it last?" - with a simple response. Beanie Babies can last as long as Barbies. (*Forever? Maybe!*) In short, there is no reason for kids to stop buying the most *irresistible,* and the best $5 - $7 toy ever made. (Note: A perfect 1959 Barbie Doll recently fetched $8,800 at auction!)

Beanie Baby Bandwagon. Seems like everyone has a Beanie product these days. Here is General Mills' entry: "Breakfast Babies," a Lucky Charms premium.

Here Today - Gone Tamagotchi?

On May 26, 1997, *People* magazine ran a full-page story on its "Trends" page announcing: "Bye-bye, Beanie Babies...The latest toy craze is a 'virtual pet' from Japan." Although no explanation was given for the predicted demise of America's most popular toy, a Tamagotchi (Bandai) vice president was quoted as saying: "We've shipped more pieces than Elmo and Beanie Babies combined." *Yeah, right!* (We'd like to see the bills of lading.)

In our experience as full-time, serious collectors for 30 years, we've seen fads come and go. After the first 5 years (Beanie Babies began in 1993), it's really unfair to call this new collectible a fad. Therefore, like our song says: "Beanie Babies Are Here To Stay!"*

Rare Ty heart button given to Ty sales representatives
(From the authors' collection)

*NOTE: Les and Sue Fox have written lyrics and music for a Beanie Baby CD to be produced by a Grammy-winning New York arranger.

The Truth About Dogs

It is said that if you take a sick dog and nurse him to health, and make him happy, and help him achieve his potential, he will never bite you. That is the principal difference between a dog and a man.

Collecting "Special" Kinds of Beanie Babies

Many people enjoy collecting Beanie Babies by the groups they belong to, such as:

 Cats   Jungle Beasts   Farm Animals

 Bunnies   Birds & Bats   Forest Creatures

 Bears   Aquatic Animals   Reptiles

It's also fun to collect Beanies by color: All red, black & white, tie-dyed, etc.

Be Original! Collect What Appeals To You!

A GUIDE TO COLLECTING

BEANIE BABIES IN 1998 (AND BEYOND)

Find any Beanie Baby bargains lately? Fat chance...with everyone in America searching high and low for extinct dinosaurs, miscellaneous jungle beasts, farm animals, exotic birds and multi-colored fish! As we noted last year, few people hit paydirt at the local flea market. But we also suggested some time-tested rules that seasoned collectors (like us) follow religiously. The first is to know your market.

For instance, when we went to press last year even we did not know the whole story about Lucky the Ladybug. In May, 1997, it was commonly believed that the only rare Lucky was the original (1994) version, the one with seven glued-on spots. We reported that this Lucky was hard to find (his spots fall off) in mint condition, and worth $100. For some strange reason, "Lucky-7" as we like to call him is not selling for a whole lot more in 1998. In fact, he's a pretty good buy right now. On the other hand, "Lucky-21" (the style with 21 spots) turns out to be the rarest of the three, and you could have "struck it rich" buying Lucky-21's at only $10 to $20 last year. We finally picked one up just before Thanksgiving for $430!

What happened? Well, it seems that for a while (in 1996) red fabric was available with lots of small black dots. However, that production run apparently didn't last long and gradually Beanie collectors (including us) began to notice that there were oodles of Lucky-11's, but very few Lucky 21's. The price of the 21-spot Lucky suddenly jumped from $10 to $20 to $50 to $100 to $200 to...$430! Now, of course, it's a little late to start accumulating Lucky-21's. However, you might still be lucky enough to stumble across one at a Beanie Baby swap meet or in a shop that just happens to have a binful of Luckies. The point is, knowledge is power.

We also mentioned in the First Edition that "it is possible that some of today's *least* popular styles could turn out to be among the most desirable from an investment aspect." Example: Grunt. Take a look at Grunt's page in the retired section. Wow! From $5 to $100+ is almost as big a jump as Lucky-21 and percentage-wise more than the Beanie Baby rarities! Why? What's the big deal with Grunt? Answer: He's scarce. And to make matters worse he was available by the thousands when we predicted he would rise in value from $5 to $40 in 10 years. As we went to press, Grunt was retired. Instantly, he became a $15-$25 toy. But who would have guessed Grunt would continue to appreciate so dramatically?

All of this surprise and intrigue is what makes collecting Beanie Babies so exciting. Where else can you be "a big spender" with only $50? Where else can your potential loss be so limited (you can always give away unwanted Beanies as birthday gifts) and your potential gain so great? Even the Dow Jones hasn't kept up with the Dow Beanie!

The Great McDonald's Opportunity

Last April, once again just as we were going to press, McDonald's staged its most successful Happy Meal give-away ever. The 10 different McDonald's Teenie Beanies (see special chapter in this book) hit the fast-food restaurants like a ton of cheese! Although this promotion was finished by May, we revealed a valuable collector's tip. We advised our readers that we had stashed away 200 McDonald's plastic garbage can banks in 1976 at 15 cents apiece. In 20 years, the price per "collectible" had appreciated to $5. We then proposed our own "theory of scarcity" that at least 90% of *almost everything* just seems to disappear within 10 years. Therefore, almost everything is worth buying as a future collectible!

If you had followed this advice independently, you could have done what we did and bought 500 Teenie Beanies at $2.00 to $2.50 each by frequenting about ten different McDonald's on a weekly basis. (Technically, the toys were free if you could find a way to freeze the food. We still have some Hamburger Happy Meals in the basement refrigerator.) But even if you missed this great opportunity to invest in "cheap McDonald's stock," you still have a chance to cash in on the future by picking up a few 10-piece sets at current prices. Take our word for it. Prices aren't going down. In fact, as soon as McDonald's begins its second Teenie Beanie promotion in 1998, the first 10 toys are headed for $25 apiece.

But here's the real scoop. Some of the new toys are going to be even better values than the old! Why? Because, according to our research, McDonald's manufactures uneven amounts of each Teenie Beanie. So keep your eyes open, and try to figure out which 1998 Teenie Beanies are hardest to get. (A Teenie Beanie Peace is like money in the bank!)

What we're trying to tell you is that when it comes to collecting, nothing is obvious. Even with this book, you have to learn to read between the lines. First do your homework, then burn up a little old-fashioned shoe leather and, finally, go against the crowd. Our best Teenie Beanie investment was scoffing up 50 of the special "Ty" Happy Meal bags, which were available at no charge. These are now very scarce collector's items. So is the beautiful Teenie Beanie store display.

Other "Sleepers"

Basically, if you can afford to do this, simply putting away five or ten of each and every new Beanie Baby in super mint condition isn't a bad idea. Like we said, the worst you can do is eventually give away "extra" Beanies as inexpensive gifts. (There's no better buy in America!) But you just might wind up with a few big winners, like Grunt.

Original 9 Beanies: Flash, Patti, Splash, Spot, Legs, Squealer, Cubbie, Chocolate, Pinchers

A better strategy, we think, is to study the market and figure out which toys don't seem to be in strong demand. This involves a little more work, but who said life was easy? Check in with local Beanie dealers from time to time and ask which toys don't seem to be moving. (Lately, all of the new releases have been so hot that no one can keep them in stock, but this is bound to change.) Also, use your own eyeballs and note which Beanies seem to be sitting around, as "leftovers." For instance, of the May, 1997 releases Chip the Cat and Jolly the Walrus have not received the high level of attention accorded to Baldy, Doodles (Strut), Blizzard and Roary. So while we'd certainly hang on to some of the best sellers, years from now you're liable to wish that you had stocked up on some of the slower movers. Check out our nutty Beanie Hunter Tips for some hidden sound advice.

Among "underpriced" toys, we also like the original 9 Beanies with their original, first generation hang tags. Throughout this year's edition, we note that such collector's items are a good buy at $40 to $50. Good observation, but now try to buy 'em! (Hint: You can't. Only a small percentage of these Beanies were issued with the early tags, and most were cut off and discarded.) And how do we know this? Experience. As serious Beanie collectors, we've been trying to buy the original 9 with their original tags (at *any* reasonable price) with little luck.

The Bottom Line

The bottom line in Beanie Baby collecting is, obviously, not to go too crazy over anything. Sooner or later, if the hobby sticks around (as we suspect it will), you'll get your chance to buy every Beanie Baby animal, including a camel. When? Whenever Ty decides to make an interesting new version of Humphrey, in a different color, with a catchy new name like Sandy or Egypt. So don't fret if you don't have enough money for a Mercedes *and* a complete set of Beanie Babies. Or if you missed your chance to buy twenty examples of a retired Beanie Baby accidentally left on a store shelf until 10 minutes before your return. (This is a good way to make a killing, if you're quick and cold-blooded.) Remember, every dog has his day, and we'll all get our chance to do something brilliant sooner or later.

28

A herd of Humphreys. (4 raffled during October 1997 Beanie Baby Extravaganza Weekend.)

For information purposes only, we have listed below "The 10 Rarest Beanie Babies" from last year's Beanie Baby Handbook. Compare 1997 values with current 1998 values. Then ask yourself what you honestly believe will happen to these prices in the future. Many people think prices are highly inflated. (What isn't these days?) Others think these collectible toys are a safe bet. After all, it only takes one more genuine collector to make prices rise.

Where to go from here is entirely up to you. To our average reader, we highly recommend taking a conservative approach. The most money you can lose buying something for $5.00 is $5.00 (plus lost interest!) If twenty $5.00 toys double in value, you've done just as well as if a $100.00 toy doubles. Which is not to say that $5 toys are better buys than $100 toys. That is a decision you'll have to make yourself. As collectors, Sue and I always found that collecting "the best" offers the most pride of ownership and the greatest financial rewards. That rule has applied to everything from oil paintings to wood carvings to Coca Cola collectibles, to you name it. Of course, there is one other factor to consider. There has never been anything quite like Beanie Babies before. And there may never be again.

The 10 Rarest Beanie Babies

	1997 Value	1998 Value
1. SPOT (Without spot)	$1,200	$1,500
2. PEANUT (Dark blue)	1,500	2,500
3. QUACKER (No wings)	1,000	1,500
4. ZIP (All black)	1,000	1,250
5. PATTI (Maroon)	750	750
6. CHILLY	750	1,000
7. NIP (All gold)	750	750
8. HUMPHREY	650	1,000
9. PEKING	500	1,000
10. TEDDY BROWN (Old Face)	600	1,000

Rare Beanie Baby errors. (From the authors' collection)

Lefty without flag *Mystic without tail* *Righty with upside-down flag*

Everything You Need To Know About...
BEANIE BABY TAGS

Beanie Baby tags may seem complicated, so let's simplify. First, other than for proper references, most collectors don't care about a Beanie Baby's "rear end" or "tush" tag...as long as it's intact! The most important tag on a Beanie Baby is the cardboard heart-shaped "Ty" tag, also known as a "hang" tag.

First Generation Tag (1993-1994)

The first generation hang tag is a single tag. It's also the only version in the shape of a full heart. This tag appeared on the original 9 and other early Beanie Babies. Most were detached and discarded, so these tags are collector's items.

Second Generation Tag (1994-1995)

The second generation hang tag is a double tag. Like its successors, the left part of the heart is missing. This tag is folded into a booklet of two attached hearts. On the right-hand heart is a "To / From" section for gift use.

Third Generation Tag (1995-1996)

The third generation hang tag is the same booklet format with fatter lettering. Inside is the same "To / From" set-up and, as before, the Style Number.

Fourth Generation Tag (1996-1997)

The fourth generation hang tag is the same as the third generation tag with 5 noteworthy changes: A poem, a birthday, a yellow star, no black outline on "Ty," and Ty's website address.

Fifth Generation Tag (1998-Current)

The newest Ty hang tag contains very subtle changes. The interior type style (& inside the star) is new, the birthday is spelled out and the Style # has been omitted.

4 & 5

In general, Beanie Babies without hang tags are worth only 50% to 75% of their full value. Creased tags also depreciate the value of a toy. In the case of important rarities demand for mint condition examples sometimes minimizes the discount. Plastic tag protectors are the best way to prevent tag damage.

In response to the hundreds of questions people ask about tag errors, here's a good general answer. Only a tiny percentage of all Beanie Baby collectors care about tag errors. Mistagged Beanies are not especially valuable. A tush mis-tag is better than a hang mis-tag, but as a rule tag errors add only $10 to $25 to the value of a toy. On the other hand, rare and highly collectible tags (like "Brownie") are extremely valuable.

IMPORTANT: Beanies with "early" tags are worth $25 to $100 more.

Introducing...

The Beanie Baby
Collection

of

Les, Sue and Jamie Fox

The "Current" Beanies
Introduction

This section of The Beanie Baby Handbook contains the 82 Beanie Babies currently in production by Ty, Inc.

As experienced Beanie collectors already know, the fact that a Beanie Baby is in "current production" does not necessarily mean you can easily obtain one at the original issue price of $5 to $7. As noted on the page for Peace the tie-dyed Bear, very few shoppers have been able to buy Peace for less than $40 to $75. Peace was "officially issued" on May 11, 1997 but none were available for at least a month. Last May we tried unsuccessfully to purchase Peace for $250 to photograph! Shortly thereafter, Peace turned up in England and Disney World, as well as in large and small toy stores and gift shops, without any rhyme or reason whatsoever. A similar situation occurred with the October 1st releases, for which many collectors paid $25 to $50 apiece!

The point is, some "current Beanies" are readily available (as all should be) and some are not. This is only one of the many reasons Beanie Babies remain a mysterious commodity. In our opinion, until Beanies there has never been a mass produced $5 toy which could be purchased at its full retail price (or higher) and instantly resold for up to 10 times that price. This has to be one of the great marketing paradoxes of the 20th Century. The Ty company currently limits authorized dealers to 36 units of each style monthly (sometimes less), and who knows what anyone will actually receive?

In any event, for each of the so-called "current" Beanie Babies you will find the following information:

(1) **A Name**.

(2) **A Birthday**. Assigned only to Beanie styles accompanied by a "fourth generation" heart tag. (See Tag page in "Collecting" chapter.) This birthday does not coincide with the release date of the toy. It is usually earlier.

(3) **A "Tag Poem."** (Again, only fourth generation toys have one.)

(4) **Total Born**. Strictly our own "unofficial" estimate. For recent releases, production figures may increase as more toys are manufactured.

(5) **Estimated Survival In 10 Years**. How many toys we think will still exist in the year 2008. (10%) Of these, a smaller percentage will be mint with tags.

(6) **Likely To Be Retired**. Our guess as to when a current Beanie will be sent to "Beanie Baby Heaven." (Beanies, of course, live forever.)

(7) **Style Number**. The manufacturer's stock number. We can't figure out the logical sequence, and some Beanies have duplicate style numbers.

(8) **Issue Price**. Generally, new issues retail for $5 to $7.

(9) **1998 Value**. What you might expect to pay today. However, as soon as a Beanie Baby is "retired" (or even if people suspect it will be retired soon), expect 1998 value to jump.

(10) **Year 2008**. What we think a Mint Condition specimen (with mint tags) will be worth in 10 years.

(11) **Our Recommendation**. We either like Beanies, or love them!

(12) **Beanie Hunter Tips**. A combination of sound collector advice, animal trivia, corny jokes, cute concepts for kids to ponder and totally ridiculous statements. Take these for what they're worth.

NOTE: A yellow star identifies the "Original 9" Beanie Babies created in 1993. Some are current, some are retired. All are incredibly cute and cuddly.

BALDY

(The Eagle)

Hair on his head is quite scant

Hair in his eyes would make it hard to see!

We suggest Baldy get a transplant

Watching over the land of the free

 Birthday: February 17, 1996

TOTAL BORN: 1,000,000
Est. Survival (2008): 100,000

Likely to be Retired: 2000
Style #4074

ISSUE PRICE	$5.00 - $7.00
1998 Value	$5.00 - $7.00
Year 2008 (est.)	$60.00

 Recommended

BEANIE HUNTER TIPS: Styled after Caw and Kiwi (both retired), Baldy sports the traditional Beanie Baby bird form including three-prong tail feathers. The American Eagle is our nation's monetary and military symbol. Therefore, we consider it downright unpatriotic if not treasonous to refuse to enlist Baldy in your collection.

BATTY
(The Bat)

Bats may make some people jitter

This Beanie Bat would love to hug you.

Please don't be scared of this critter

If you're lonely or have nothing to do

 Birthday: October 29, 1996

TOTAL BORN:	500,000	**Likely to be Retired: 1999**
Est. Survival (2008):	50,000	**Style #4035**

ISSUE PRICE	$5.00 - $7.00
1998 Value	$5.00 - $25.00
Year 2008 (est.)	$100.00

Highly
Recommended

BEANIE HUNTER TIPS: Like Radar, we're guessing that Batty's status as a "current" Beanie Baby will be short lived. Batty is the first Beanie utilizing velcro tabs. This allows the toy to be posed in a nocturnal position. Regrettably, "Count Batty" was largely unavailable for Halloween '97, but should be venturing out of his cave in droves come next October! Batty will probably prove more popular with boys, which means he will not be treated too gently.

BERNIE
(The St. Bernard)

This little dog can't wait to grow

He doesn't know how to rescue himself!

To rescue people lost in the snow

Don't let him out - keep him on your shelf!

 Birthday: October 3, 1996

TOTAL BORN:	2,000,000	Likely to be Retired: 2000
Est. Survival (2008):	200,000	Style #4109

ISSUE PRICE	$5.00 - $7.00
1998 Value	$5.00 - $7.00
Year 2008 (est.)	$60.00

 Recommended

BEANIE HUNTER TIPS: Although Bernie the rescue dog turns up in Beanie shops now and then, he's one of the less frequently seen pooches. We think you'll have a couple of more years to pick up Bernie at the original issue price, but the Ty company is full of surprises. If Bernie suddenly disappears from the scene, don't expect us to come to your rescue!

✿ **BLACKIE** ✿
(The Circus Bear)

Living in a national park

Now they play when it's sunny!

He only played after dark

Then he met his friend Cubbie

🎂 **Birthday: July 15, 1994**

TOTAL BORN: 3,000,000

Est. Survival (2008): 300,000

Likely to be Retired: 1998

Style #4011

ISSUE PRICE	$5.00 - $7.00
1998 Value	$5.00 - $15.00
Year 2008 (est.)	$75.00

👍👍 **Highly Recommended**

BEANIE HUNTER TIPS: Repeating our earlier advice, Blackie could be retired at any time! Please note that we have nicknamed Blackie "The Circus Bear" to correspond with one of our new Beanie Baby songs. Don't be surprised to find Blackie hanging around your local ice cream parlor. His favorite flavor is vanilla, so please remember to wipe his chin before he retires! (NOTE: Blackie is rare with a third generation hang tag, worth $40.)

☼ **BLIZZARD** ☼
(The White Tiger)

In the mountains, where it's snowy and cold

Of all the tigers, she is most rare

Lives a beautiful tiger, I've been told

Black and white, she's hard to compare

 Birthday: December 12, 1996

TOTAL BORN:	1,000,000	**Likely to be Retired: 1998**	
Est. Survival (2008):	100,000		**Style #4163**

ISSUE PRICE	**$5.00 - $7.00**
1998 Value	**$5.00 - $15.00**
Year 2008 (est.)	**$85.00**

 Highly Recommended

BEANIE HUNTER TIPS: Since his escape from Siegfried and Roy, Blizzard has been an elusive Beanie to track down and capture. As you know the rarity of a white tiger is legendary, especially in the Beanie Baby jungle. (NOTE: Blizzard has the same blue eyes as Mystic and Nanook.) Considering all of the controversy which surrounds him, we highly doubt that Blizzard will be around in two years.

BONES
(The Dog)

Bones is a dog that loves to chew

But that all stopped, when his teeth fell out!

Chairs and a table and a smelly old shoe

"You're so destructive," all would shout

Birthday: January 18, 1994

TOTAL BORN:	6,000,000	Likely to be Retired: 1998
Est. Survival (2008):	600,000	Style #4001

ISSUE PRICE	$5.00 - $7.00
1998 Value	$5.00 - $15.00
Year 2008 (est.)	$60.00

 Recommended

BEANIE HUNTER TIPS: We really thought Bones would be history in 1997, but due to his great popularity he's still sniffing out new collectors. Now is the time for all good Beanie Hunters to come to the aid of their canines! Make no bones about it, this pup's a future champion!

☼ BONGO ☼
(The Monkey)

Bongo the monkey lives in a tree

One of these days he will be a big star!

He's the happiest monkey that will ever see

In his spare time he plays the guitar

🎂 Birthday: August 17, 1995

TOTAL BORN:	5,000,000	**Likely to be Retired: 1998**
Est. Survival (2008):	500,000	**Style #4067**

ISSUE PRICE	**$5.00 - $7.00**
1998 Value	**$5.00 - $15.00**
Year 2008 (est.)	**$60.00**

 Recommended

BEANIE HUNTER TIPS: Bongo is an interesting primate. A prototype of Bongo as a red monkey with a cream colored face appeared in an early Ty illustration. (We'd love to buy one for our collection.) This toy was never released. First Bongo was named Nana (for "banana") and is worth $1,200 with the Nana hang tag. Then, for a while, Bongo had a dark brown tail (a good buy at $20 - $30.) Now it's about time for Bongo to grab a vine and do his famous vanishing act!

☼ BRITANNIA ☼
(The Bear)

🎂 **Birthday: 1997**

TOTAL BORN:	100,000	Likely to be Retired: 1999
Est. Survival (2008):	10,000	Style #: None

ISSUE PRICE	$5.00 - $7.00
1998 Value	$50.00 - $75.00
Year 2008 (est.)	$500.00

 Highly Recommended

BEANIE HUNTER TIPS: Like Maple, Britannia the Bear is an all exclusive Beanie Baby not sold directly into the US market. In order to get one of these must-have teddies it helps to have friends in faraway places. Or, instead of eating out in fancy restaurants, why not save up for a trip to London? (Caution: Don't lose Britannia in the pea soup fog!)

BRUNO
(The Bull Terrier)

Bruno the dog thinks he's a brute

NEW FOR '98

And everyone says, "Oh, how darling!"

But all the other Beanie Babies think he's cute

He growls at his tail and runs in a ring

 Birthday: September 9, 1997

TOTAL BORN:	250,000	Likely to be Retired: 2000
Est. Survival (2008):	25,000	Style #: None

ISSUE PRICE	$5.00 - $7.00
1998 Value	$5.00 - $12.00
Year 2008 (est.)	$60.00

 Highly Recommended

BEANIE HUNTER TIPS: Bred to be the ultimate fighting dog, Bruno is a second cousin of Spuds McKenzie, the former Budweiser mascot. This pup has not yet fully developed his muscularity. By the end of the year, you would be wise to avoid getting a thumb caught in Bruno's incredibly powerful jaws, which lock on a target and may never release! (NOTE: Bruno is more of a lover than a fighter.)

CHIP

☼ ☼

(The Calico Cat)

Black and gold, brown and white

On anyone else it would be a disaster!

The shades of her coat are quite a sight

At mixing her colors she was a master

🎂 **Birthday: January 26, 1996**

TOTAL BORN:	**1,000,000**	**Likely to be Retired: 2000**
Est. Survival (2008):	**100,000**	**Style #4121**

ISSUE PRICE	**$5.00 - $7.00**
1998 Value	**$5.00 - $7.00**
Year 2008 (est.)	**$60.00**

👍 Recommended

BEANIE HUNTER TIPS: Issued in May, 1997. As we predicted last year, the next new cat was indeed a Calico! Since Ty Warner is a cat lover whose first plush toys were Himalayans, we respectfully request a Himalayan Beanie Baby! (Second choice, a Persian.) According to experts, cats utilize 16 distinct sounds to communicate. The authors placed Nip, Zip, Flip, Snip and Chip in a private room with recording devices. You won't believe what "catty" cats will say behind your back!

☼ **CHOCOLATE** ☼
(The Moose)

Licorice, gum and peppermint candy

Can you guess his favorite sweet?

This moose always has these handy

But there is one more thing he likes to eat

ORIGINAL 1

 Birthday: April 27, 1993

TOTAL BORN: 5,000,000	**Likely to be Retired: 1998**
Est. Survival (2008): 500,000	**Style #4015**

ISSUE PRICE	**$5.00 - $7.00**
1998 Value	**$5.00 - $15.00**
Year 2008 (est.)	**$75.00**

 Highly Recommended

BEANIE HUNTER TIPS: As you can see, Chocolate has been around "forever" in Beanie Baby years. He is ranked "the most popular" Beanie in many surveys. Like all of the earliest "original nine," the Chocolates were issued with a first generation tag. (Highly recommended at $40 - $50.) Eventually, a cuddly reindeer will take over as the Beanie Baby with antlers. Don't you find it amusing that "Chocolate" comes after "Chip"?

✿ CLAUDE ✿
(The Tie-Dyed Crab)

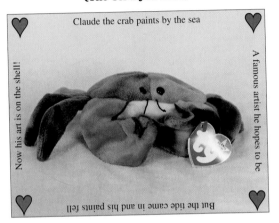

Claude the crab paints by the sea

Now his art is on the shell!

A famous artist he hopes to be

But the tide came in and his paints fell

 Birthday: September 3, 1996

TOTAL BORN:	1,000,000	**Likely to be Retired: 1999**	
Est. Survival (2008):	100,000	**Style #4083**	

ISSUE PRICE	$5.00 - $7.00
1998 Value	$5.00 - $15.00
Year 2008 (est.)	$75.00

 Highly Recommended

BEANIE HUNTER TIPS: This colorful crustacean has captured the hearts of both boys and girls since coming out of his shell in May, 1997. Because tie-dyed Beanies are among the most collectible in the series, don't expect Claude to be around too long. Reflecting aquatic surface colors of rust, purple and green, Claude the crab is deceptive. In fact, he'd rather spend time in a kid's room than buried in sand or sea.

✿ CONGO ✿
(The Gorilla)

Black as night and fierce is he

He's related to our friend Bongo!

On the ground or in a tree

Strong and mighty as the Congo

 Birthday: November 9, 1996

TOTAL BORN:	3,000,000	**Likely to be Retired: 1998**
Est. Survival (2008):	300,000	**Style #4160**

ISSUE PRICE	$5.00 - $7.00
1998 Value	$5.00 - $15.00
Year 2008 (est.)	$60.00

 Recommended

BEANIE HUNTER TIPS: Normally the strong, silent type (except when beating his chest, a natural instinct), Congo is not crazy about gorilla jokes. Example: Which Beanie Baby do you give to a 600-pound gorilla? (Answer: Your whole collection!) Fortunately, Congo is a vegetarian, so you can crack all the dumb gorilla jokes you want.

☼ CRUNCH ☼
(The Shark)

What's for breakfast? What's for lunch?

That's the reason we named him Crunch!

Yum! Delicious! Munch, munch, munch!

He's eating everything by the bunch

Birthday: January 13, 1996

TOTAL BORN: 2,000,000
Est. Survival (2008): 200,000

Likely to be Retired: 1998
Style #4130

ISSUE PRICE	**$5.00 - $7.00**
1998 Value	**$5.00 - $15.00**
Year 2008 (est.)	**$75.00**

 Highly Recommended

BEANIE HUNTER TIPS: The red, white and blue-grey Crunch continues to be the ultimate Beanie Baby predator! (Shark trivia: Sharks must swim constantly, or they will sink. They also have superb eyesight as well as an asymmetrical tail, and rather pointy teeth.) We think Crunch's anticipated 1997 retirement has been postponed until 1998, which is why Crunch often hums "Mack The Knife."

☼ CURLY ☼
(The Brown Bear)

A bear so cute with hair that's curly

He will be a friend to you!

You will love and want him surely

To this bear always be true

 Birthday: April 12, 1996

TOTAL BORN:	**2,000,000**	**Likely to be Retired: 1998**
Est. Survival (2008):	**200,000**	**Style #4052**

ISSUE PRICE	**$5.00 - $7.00**
1998 Value	**$5.00 - $15.00**
Year 2008 (est.)	**$75.00**

 Highly Recommended

BEANIE HUNTER TIPS: As of February, 1998, Curly was one of three pre-1997 Beanie Baby teddy bears not yet retired. Seen in stores far less frequently than many in-production Beanies, the nappy-skinned Curly is certainly one of the most adorable $5 toys ever made. Watch for Curly to star in a Sunday Night TV Special entitled: "Goldilocks And The Three Beanie Bears."

☼ DAISY ☼
(The Black & White Cow)

Daisy drinks milk each night

What a way for your day to begin!

So her coat is shiny and bright

Milk is good for your hair and skin

Birthday: May 10, 1994

TOTAL BORN:	4,000,000	Likely to be Retired: 1998
Est. Survival (2008):	400,000	Style #4006

ISSUE PRICE	$5.00 - $7.00
1998 Value	$5.00 - $15.00
Year 2008 (est.)	$75.00

Highly Recommended

BEANIE HUNTER TIPS: Last year we predicted that Daisy would be the first retired cow would be retired, but it was Bessie! This year, look for Daisy to moo-ve out of the "current" Beanie category. Who will replace this two-tone beauty? We're still waiting for Bluebelle.

☼ DERBY ☼
(The Horse)

All the other horses used to tattle

Just so Derby can be with you!

Because Derby never wore his saddle

He left the stables, and the horses too

🎂 **Birthday: September 16, 1995**

TOTAL BORN: 5,000,000
Est. Survival (2008): 500,000

Likely to be Retired: 1998
Style #4008

ISSUE PRICE	$5.00 - $7.00
1998 Value	$5.00 - $15.00
Year 2008 (est.)	$75.00

 Highly Recommended

BEANIE HUNTER TIPS: A horse's age is determined by inspecting its teeth. (Caution: Buy Derby quickly and don't look a gift horse in the mouth!) At age three, Derby is getting old in Beanie years. Hey! Who's that galloping out of the starting box? A red and white horse? Neigh! (Get it?) See also: Retired Derby. Derby's fabric matches Bones. (NOTE: The 1998 version of this dapper trotter features a white marking on Derby's forehead.)

DOBY
(The Doberman)

This dog is little but he has might

Until he sees it's time to protect you!

Keep him close when you sleep at night

He lays around with nothing to do

 Birthday: October 9, 1996

TOTAL BORN:	2,000,000	**Likely to be Retired: 2000**
Est. Survival (2008):	200,000	**Style #4110**

ISSUE PRICE	**$5.00 - $7.00**
1998 Value	**$5.00 - $7.00**
Year 2008 (est.)	**$60.00**

 Recommended

BEANIE HUNTER TIPS: Except for coloration, Doby and Bernie could be twins. This means, it could be bad luck (and quite unsociable) to own one without the other. Who can resist that immature, innocent, take-me-home-and-love-me puppy face? Surely not the millions of kids (and adults) who collect Beanie dogs. By the way, we've moved up Doby's retirement from 2002 to 2000. If you have room in your house, pick up a pair of dobermans today.

☼ DOODLE/STRUT ☼
(The Rooster)

Listen closely to "Cock-a-doodle-doo"

We have lots to do, get out of bed!

What's the rooster saying to you?

Hurry, wake up sleepy head

 Birthday: March 8, 1996

TOTAL BORN: 1,000,000   **Likely to be Retired:** 2000
Est. Survival (2008): 100,000   **Style #4171**

	Doodle	Strut
ISSUE PRICE	$5.00 - $7.00	$5.00 - $7.00
1998 Value	$35.00	$5.00 - $10.00
Year 2008 (est.)	$150.00	$75.00

👍👍 **Highly Recommended**

BEANIE HUNTER TIPS: Due to a potential conflict with Chicken Fil-A, Doodle's name was changed to "Strut" within weeks of his release in May, 1997. (NOTE: In our 1997 book, we predicted the debut of a rooster named Doodle.) As soon as this proud, tie-dyed fowl emerged from the hen house, his price escalated from $5 to as high as $40. In 10 years, the original version may well be worth $150. Luckily for us, we came across a gaggle of Doodles at only $6 each at a local craft store. (See back cover)

DOTTY
(The Dalmatian)

The Beanies all thought it was a big joke

So now the Beanies call her Dotty!

While writing her tag, their ink pen broke

She got in the way, and got all spotty

 **Birthday: October 17, 1996**

TOTAL BORN: 1,000,000   Likely to be Retired: 1998
Est. Survival (2008): 100,000   Style #4100

ISSUE PRICE	$5.00 - $7.00
1998 Value	$5.00 - $15.00
Year 2008 (est.)	$60.00

 Highly
Recommended

BEANIE HUNTER TIPS: In 1997, the authors suggested that Sparky the Dalmatian's retirement could come as early as it did. Sparky was retired on May 11, 1997. We have a strong hunch that Beanie collectors will be treated to a new Dalmatian every year until there are 101 varieties. Let's see if we're right by the year 2097!

 54

EARS

☼　☼

(The Bunny)

He's been eating carrots so long

Until the doctor gave him glasses!

Didn't understand what was wrong

Couldn't see the board during classes

🎂 **Birthday: April 18, 1995**

TOTAL BORN: 4,000,000   Likely to be Retired: 1998
Est. Survival (2008): 400,000   Style #4018

ISSUE PRICE	$5.00 - $7.00
1998 Value	$5.00 - $15.00
Year 2008 (est.)	$60.00

 Highly
Recommended

BEANIE HUNTER TIPS: For some strange reason, the Ty company seems to have made twice as many examples of Ears recently compared to the three "sit-up" bunnies. Is this because Ears is so popular, or is the fabric for the other toys harder to come by? Did you know that rabbits can reproduce several times a year with up to six bunnies per litter? At this rate, the number of live rabbits may someday approach the number of Beanie Baby Bunnies!

ECHO
(The Dolphin)

Echo the dolphin lives in the sea

"I'm so glad to have you around!"

Playing with her friends, like you and me

Through the waves she echoes the sound

🎂 **Birthday: December 21, 1996**

TOTAL BORN:	1,000,000	**Likely to be Retired: 2000**
Est. Survival (2008):	100,000	**Style #4084**

ISSUE PRICE	$5.00 - $7.00
1998 Value	$5.00 - $7.00
Year 2008 (est.)	$60.00

👍 Recommended

BEANIE HUNTER TIPS: By any chance, do you happen to have an Echo with a "Waves" hang tag and/or tush tag? Join the crowd! Thousands of people were surprised to discover this massive error in May, 1997 which was corrected only after a huge first shipment left the factory. (Value of the error: $10 - $30 if you can find a buyer.) If you plan to lounge around in shark-infested waters, better bring along a bunch of Echos. A group of dolphins can ward off sharks with a barrage of snout butts!

✿ **FLEECE** ✿
(The Lamb)

Fleece would like to sing a lullaby

Her song will leave you nothing to fear.

But please be patient, she's rather shy

When you sleep, keep her by your ear.

 Birthday: March 21, 1996

TOTAL BORN: 2,000,000
Est. Survival (2008): 200,000

Likely to be Retired: **1998**

Style #4125

ISSUE PRICE	$5.00 -	$7.00
1998 Value	$5.00 -	$15.00
Year 2008 (est.)		$60.00

👍👍 Highly Recommended

BEANIE HUNTER TIPS: Following in Chops' soft footsteps, this delicately featured off-white, nappy-coated lamb may not be around for long. In fact, we've seen very few of these sweet little faces on store shelves lately. One of the four Beanie Babies with a non-plush body (which includes Scotty, Tuffy and Curly), Fleece is a "shear" delight to have as a pet on the farm or in an apartment.

✿ FLOPPITY ✿
(The Lilac Bunny)

Floppity hops from here to there

All dressed up and nowhere to go!

Searching for eggs without a care

Lavendar coat from head to toe

Birthday: May 28, 1996

TOTAL BORN: 2,000,000	Likely to be Retired: 1998
Est. Survival (2008): 200,000	Style #4118

ISSUE PRICE	$5.00 - $7.00
1998 Value	$5.00 - $15.00
Year 2008 (est.)	$75.00

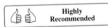

Highly
Recommended

BEANIE HUNTER TIPS: This enchanting lilac bunny is still difficult to find, even during the holidays! Like most Beanie aficionados, we're hoping that Ty's current rabbits will be replaced with "offspring" in some exciting new colors. If we don't see some new styles by next year, we'll be hopping mad! (NOTE: A prototype of Floppity, very similar to the finished product, was discovered in England. It was sold in an internet auction for $1,400.)

☼ **FRECKLES** ☼
(The Leopard)

♥ From the trees he hunts his prey ♥

Look real close, he's no mirage!

In the night and in the day

♥ He's the King of camouflage ♥

🎂 **Birthday: June 3, 1996**

TOTAL BORN:	3,000,000	**Likely to be Retired: 1998**
Est. Survival (2008):	300,000	**Style #4066**

ISSUE PRICE	$5.00 - $7.00
1998 Value	$5.00 - $15.00
Year 2008 (est.)	$60.00

👍👍 **Highly Recommended**

BEANIE HUNTER TIPS: In researching the history of the feline species, we learned that cats have been around for some 40 million years. Freckles, on the other hand, may not be around for more than 40 months before he is retired. His "faux leopard" coat is very much in vogue these days, but remember that Freckles is a carnivore. Keep him away from your Quarter Pounder.

59

☼ GOBBLES ☼
(The Turkey)

Gobbles the turkey loves to eat

If she eats too much her tummy will bulge!

Once a year she has a feast

I have a secret I'd like to divulge

🎂 **Birthday: November 27, 1996**

TOTAL BORN:	**500,000**	**Likely to be Retired: 1998**
Est. Survival (2008):	**50,000**	**Style #4034**

ISSUE PRICE	**$5.00 - $7.00**
1998 Value	**$5.00 - $25.00**
Year 2008 (est.)	**$150.00**

 Highly Recommended

BEANIE HUNTER TIPS: Gobbles is one of the elusive October, 1997 "Holiday" releases. Due to his elaborate construction, we have a sneaking suspicion that something controversial is destined to affect Gobbles' availability and to increase his future value. Don't be a "turkey" yourself... fill your Beanie Baby treasure chests with as many $5 - $7 Gobbles as you can stuff in. Then, just hang onto them for a rainy Thanksgiving.

☼ GRACIE ☼
(The Swan)

As a duckling, she was confused

Now the most beautiful swan at Ty!

Birds on the lake were quite amused

Poking fun until she would cry

 Birthday: June 17, 1996

TOTAL BORN: 2,000,000   **Likely to be Retired: 1998**
Est. Survival (2008):   200,000   **Style #4126**

ISSUE PRICE	$5.00 - $7.00
1998 Value	$5.00 - $15.00
Year 2008 (est.)	$75.00

☝ Recommended

BEANIE HUNTER TIPS: When Lucy the Goose makes her introduction (Lucy is our own idea), Gracie will be long gone! In fact, Gracie may turn out to be the swan who laid the golden egg since she has never been very popular. Consequently, the rarity of Gracie may be very underrated and within 10 years collectors may pay dearly for a clean, white waterfowl to complete their collections.

HADPPY ☼

(The Lavender Hippo)

Happy the Hippo loves to wade

You know he's happy without a doubt!

In the river and in the shade

When Happy shoots water out of his snout

 Birthday: February 25, 1994

TOTAL BORN: 3,000,000	**Likely to be Retired: 1998**
Est. Survival (2008): 300,000	**Style #4061**

ISSUE PRICE	**$5.00 - $7.00**
1998 Value	**$5.00 - $15.00**
Year 2008 (est.)	**$60.00**

 Highly Recommended

BEANIE HUNTER TIPS: Happy, the original grey hippopotaumus (See Retired) was issued in 1994 with a rare first generation hang tag. (All early tagged toys are now highly recommended at $40 - $50.) To repeat an interesting bit of animal trivia, a hippo is as long around its middle as it is from end to end. Two of the neatest features of Happy are his tiny ears and his petite beady black eyes set into a heavily bean-stuffed head. We're not quite sure if Happy's mouth is where it "seams" to be, but somehow Happy always seems to be smiling!

☼ **HIPPITY** ☼
(The Mint Bunny)

Hippity is a cute little bunny

Sniffing a flower here and there!

Dressed in green, he looks quite funny

Twitching his nose in the air

 Birthday: June 1, 1996

TOTAL BORN:	1,000,000	Likely to be Retired: 1998
Est. Survival (2008):	100,000	Style #4119

ISSUE PRICE	$5.00 - $7.00
1998 Value	$5.00 - $25.00
Year 2008 (est.)	$125.00

 Highly Recommended

BEANIE HUNTER TIPS: We still haven't seen an abundance of Hippity's, so we have not increased the relatively scarce mint-bunny's production figure. In our humble opinion, all of Ty's silly wabbits will be 24-carrot retirements before you can say, "What's up, doc?"

HISSY
(The Snake)

Curled and coiled and ready to play

NEW FOR '98

Then stay with you through thick and thin!

He waits for you patiently every day

He'll keep his best friend but not his skin

Birthday: April 4, 1997

TOTAL BORN:	250,000	**Likely to be Retired:**	1999
Est. Survival (2008):	25,000	**Style #:**	None

ISSUE PRICE	$5.00 - $7.00
1998 Value	$5.00 - $25.00
Year 2008 (est.)	$250.00

 Highly Recommended

BEANIE HUNTER TIPS: Bearing a close resemblance to the rare retired Slither, Hissy the Snake is likely to be in tremendous demand throughout 1998. (We're personally stashing away two dozen Hissy's!) As you probably know, snakes shed their skin several times a year. If this happens to Hissy, don't be surprised to find Slither underneath! Humans have always feared snakes as a symbol of evil. Not his one. But just to be safe, feed him table scraps instead of apples!

☼ **HOPPITY** ☼
(The Rose Bunny)

Hopscotch is what she likes to play

She likes to play, rain or shine!

If you don't join in, she'll hop away

So play a game if you have the time

🎂 Birthday: April 3, 1996

TOTAL BORN: 2,000,000	**Likely to be Retired: 1998**
Est. Survival (2008): 200,000	**Style #4117**

ISSUE PRICE	**$5.00 - $7.00**
1998 Value	**$5.00 - $15.00**
Year 2008 (est.)	**$75.00**

👍👍 Highly Recommended

BEANIE HUNTER TIPS: We beg to differ with Rosie Wells, who considers the rose-colored rabbit the scarcest of the three pastel bunnies. (We think Hippity is scarcer.) On the other hand, like all Beanie lovers, we recommend that your Easter basket include at least one pair of perfect condition Hoppitys, Hippitys, Floppitys, and of course Ears! There are an awful lot of Ty bunny look-alikes in the marketplace, but only these guys truly deserve to be in your garden of delights!

IGGY

(The Iguana)

Sitting on a rock, basking in the sun

His life is so perfect without a care!

Is this Iguana's idea of fun

Towel and glasses, book and beach chair

Birthday: August 12, 1997

TOTAL BORN:	250,000	**Likely to be Retired: 1999**
Est. Survival (2008):	25,000	**Style #: None**

ISSUE PRICE	$5.00 - $7.00
1998 Value	$5.00 - $12.00
Year 2008 (est.)	$100.00

 Highly Recommended

BEANIE HUNTER TIPS: The ominous-looking Iggy (with yellow eyes and a sneaky smile) may be retired this year, or possibly in 1999. Primitive in form, stoic in disposition, the slow-moving iguana is a good friend to have during the mosquito season. Don't try to find Iggy's sticky-gooey tongue. It's in there, in case he spies a delectable treat...like a flying insect, or maybe your mom's eyelashes! (NOTE: Iggy and Rainbow's tags were reversed in January, 1998.)

INCH
(The Inchworm)

Inch the worm is a friend of mine

Traveling the world without a care!

He goes so slow all the time

Inching around from here to there

Birthday: September 3, 1995

TOTAL BORN: 5,000,000   Likely to be Retired: 1999
Est. Survival (2008):   500,000   **Style #4044**

ISSUE PRICE	**$5.00 - $7.00**
1998 Value	**$5.00 - $7.00**
Year 2008 (est.)	**$60.00**

 Recommended

BEANIE HUNTER TIPS: Many people use the tip of inch's tail as a yardstick to differentiate between the color of the original vs. the newer Patti the Platypus. If your Patti matches Inch's tail, you do not have the rare one! (See Retired Patti for more details.) To further confuse the issue, there are two versions of Inch! (See Retired Inch, too.) The current Inch may never be rare, but this proud little earthworm steadfastly refuses to bury his head in the soil!

INKY ☼ ☼

(The Octopus)

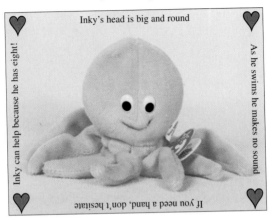

Inky's head is big and round

Inky can help because he has eight!

As he swims he makes no sound

If you need a hand, don't hesitate

🎂 **Birthday: November 29, 1994**

TOTAL BORN: 2,000,000   **Likely to be Retired: 1999**
Est. Survival (2008): 200,000   **Style #4028**

ISSUE PRICE	$5.00 - $7.00
1998 Value	$5.00 - $7.00
Year 2008 (est.)	$60.00

👍 Recommended

BEANIE HUNTER TIPS: Inky is one of the few Beanie Babies whose production figure we may have over-estimated last year. Due to a lack of demand, Inky is generally hard to find on store shelves, while collectors aggressively seek the production errors of Inky with either 7 or 9 tentacles and/or no mouth. In real life, an octopus (which has no shell) actually sprays ink to camouflage and protect itself.

68

JOLLY

(The Walrus)

Jolly the walrus is not very serious

Always happy, never sad!

He laughs and laughs until he's delirious

He often reminds me of my dad

Birthday: December 2, 1996

TOTAL BORN: 1,000,000   Likely to be Retired: 1999
Est. Survival (2008): 100,000   Style #4082

ISSUE PRICE	$5.00 - $7.00
1998 Value	$5.00 - $7.00
Year 2008 (est.)	$75.00

 Recommended

BEANIE HUNTER TIPS: As you've probably observed, Jolly is essentially Tusk with a great color change, a big, bushy mustache and a "rear fin" style modification. (Like classic Cadillacs.) Jolly's improved tusks also make it easier for him to pull himself out of the water. The newer walrus has a more authentic look and could very easily be mistaken for a genuine arctic inhabitant in January or February.

LUCKY
(The Ladybug)

Lucky the lady bug loves the lotto

Don't spend on the lotto and you'll have many!

"Someone must win" that's her motto

But save your dimes and even a penny

Birthday: May 1, 1995

TOTAL BORN:	4,000,000	**Likely to be Retired: 1999**
Est. Survival (2008):	400,000	**Style #4040**

ISSUE PRICE	**$5.00 - $7.00**
1998 Value	**$5.00 - $7.00**
Year 2008 (est.)	**$60.00**

 Recommended

BEANIE HUNTER TIPS: Of the three versions of Lucky (see also retired), Lucky #3 is the most valuable. The current Lucky is found with 11 black polkadots (as shown above). Originally, she had 7 glued on dots, but in 1996 she was temporarily made from a fabric which allowed 21 dots per insect. To farmers, ladybugs are not lucky because of their "lucky numbers" 7, 11 or 21. Ladybugs are useful to gardeners because they eat plant-killing aphids.

☼ MAPLE/PRIDE ☼
(The Canadian Teddy)

Maple the bear likes to ski

Can you guess which country he's from?

With his friends, he plays hockey

He loves his pancakes and eats every crumb

 Birthday: July 1, 1996

TOTAL BORN:	250,000	Likely to be Retired: 1998
Est. Survival (2008):	25,000	Style #4600

ISSUE PRICE	$5.00 - $7.00
1998 Value	$100.00
Year 2008 (est.)	$500.00

👍👍 **Highly Recommended**

BEANIE HUNTER TIPS: Issued in 1996 to commemorate Canadian Independence Day, Maple is produced exclusively for the Canada market. Although he is still officially "current," Maple is one of the most difficult Beanies to find in the U.S. as toys must be "imported" by enterprising Beanie brokers. The first 3,000 Maples made (value $300) had the name "Pride" on the tush tag. Maple also comes with a special ear tag (rare - value $350) which indicates support for the Canadian Special Olympics.

 71

MEL

(The Koala)

How do you name a Koala bear?

I'll name him Mel, after my favorite hunk!

It's rather tough, I do declare!

It confuses me, I get into a funk

 Birthday: January 15, 1996

TOTAL BORN:	1,000,000	**Likely to be Retired: 1999**
Est. Survival (2008):	100,000	**Style #4162**

ISSUE PRICE	**$5.00 - $7.00**
1998 Value	**$5.00 - $7.00**
Year 2008 (est.)	**$100.00**

 Highly Recommended

BEANIE HUNTER TIPS: First of all, let's get something straight. Mel the Koala is not a bear! He is a nocturnal "marsupial" (kangaroo-type pouch) who lives in eucalyptus trees in the forests of Australia. This fact, however, will not deter teddy bear collectors from putting Mel with their bears. Koalas are shy, gentle animals, which may explain why many Beanie collectors do not seem to notice Mel languishing among the hot sellers. Grab up a few Mels today, and handle with care!

MYSTIC

☼ ☼

(The Unicorn)

Once upon a time so far away

You'll see the magic in her blue eyes!

A unicorn was born one day in May

Keep Mystic with you, she's a prize

 Birthday: May 21, 1994

TOTAL BORN:	3,000,000	**Likely to be Retired: 1998**	
Est. Survival (2008):	300,000	**Style #4007**	

ISSUE PRICE	$5.00 - $7.00
1998 Value	$5.00 - $15.00
Year 2008 (est.)	$85.00

 Highly Recommended

BEANIE HUNTER TIPS: Like Derby, the "fine yarn" version of Mystic has been retired. We're guessing that the current type will soon be retired, too. As stated last year, despite his high production, Mystic is not always easy to locate, especially in white without fingerprints! According to legend, a unicorn's horn possesses magical powers. Warning: Ty, Inc. has decided to replace Mystic's tan horn with one made of Magic's iridescent fabric! (Do not pay big bucks for this toy as an error.)

☼ NANOOK ☼
(The Husky)

Nanook is a dog that loves cold weather

He runs at hearing the cry of "mush!"

To him a sled is light as a feather

Over the snow and through the slush

 Birthday: November 21, 1996

TOTAL BORN: 1,000,000	**Likely to be Retired: 2000**
Est. Survival (2008): 100,000	**Style #4104**

ISSUE PRICE	**$5.00 - $7.00**
1998 Value	**$5.00 - $7.00**
Year 2008 (est.)	**$60.00**

 Recommended

BEANIE HUNTER TIPS: Another blue-eyed Beanie, Nanook is a welcome addition to the ever-popular group of Ty dogs. It is okay to feed this hefty husky three or four times a day, but step back when he's chowing down on the kitchen floor. There is still some "wolf" in this potentially ferocious canine and he could accidentally take a tiny nip out of his owner when he's really hungry.

NUTS
(The Squirrel)

With his bushy tail, he'll scamper up a tree

Have you ever seen a squirrel like that?

The most cheerful critter you'll ever see

He's nuts about nuts, and he loves to chat

Birthday: January 21, 1996

TOTAL BORN: 3,000,000
Est. Survival (2008): 300,000

Likely to be Retired: 2000

Style #4114

ISSUE PRICE	**$5.00 - $7.00**
1998 Value	**$5.00 - $7.00**
Year 2008 (est.)	**$60.00**

Recommended

BEANIE HUNTER TIPS: Did you know that a squirrel's tail acts as a parachute when he jumps from tree to tree? We hate to admit this, but Nuts the Squirrel is actually a rodent, albeit a delightful one. More trivia: During the winter, squirrels make waterproof nests in hollow trees. Also, in mid-summer, all plush Beanie squirrels gather at the Washington Monument to celebrate America's nutty politicians.

✿ PATTI ✿
(The Platypus)

Ran into Patti one day while walking

That would explain her extra large beak!

Believe me she wouldn't stop talking

Listened and listened to her speak

ORIGINAL 9

🎂 Birthday: January 6, 1993

TOTAL BORN: 6,000,000
Est. Survival (2008): 600,000

Likely to be Retired: 1998
Style #4025

ISSUE PRICE	$5.00 - $7.00
1998 Value	$5.00 - $15.00
Year 2008 (est.)	$60.00

 Recommended

BEANIE HUNTER TIPS: While Patti is one of the highest production Beanies, she is also one of the most played-with Beanies. (See also retired Patti.) Consequently, there may be a lot fewer perfect condition Patti's floating around in 10 years than our statistics suggest. If you have the money to set aside a thousand $5 purple Patti's, you could be swimming in green! At Patti's last birthday party, she and Bucky played the Conga drum together with their wide tails.

☼ PEACE ☼
(The Tie-Dyed Bear)

All races, all colors, under the sun

Symbols of peace and love abound!

Join hands together and have some fun

Dance to the music, rock and roll is the sound

 Birthday: February 1, 1996

TOTAL BORN:	500,000	**Likely to be Retired: 1999**	
Est. Survival (2008):	50,000	**Style #4053**	

ISSUE PRICE	**$5.00 - $7.00**
1998 Value	**$5.00 - $75.00**
Year 2008 (est.)	**$200.00**

 Highly Recommended

BEANIE HUNTER TIPS: Anybody around here seen Garcia? Wow! Peace the Bear has been in production for nearly a year and trying to buy one for $5 - $7 is still a Beanie shopper's nightmare. Part of the thrill of collecting Beanie Babies is the mystique surrounding how a mass produced "$5 toy" can manage to sell for 15 times its ~~retail~~ value on the open market. Amazing! (Rumor we hope is true: McD~~onald's is~~ planning to make a Teenie Beanie Peace.) Currently the ~~biggest seller i~~n America!

☼ PEANUT ☼
(The Elephant)

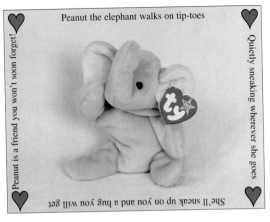

Peanut the elephant walks on tip-toes

Peanut is a friend you won't soon forget!

Quietly sneaking wherever she goes

She'll sneak up on you and a hug you will get

 Birthday: January 25, 1995

TOTAL BORN:	3,000,000	Likely to be Retired: 2001
Est. Survival (2008):	300,000	Style #4062

ISSUE PRICE	$5.00 - $7.00
1998 Value	$5.00 - $7.00
Year 2008 (est.)	$60.00

 Recommended

BEANIE HUNTER TIPS: Okay, which wise guy dyed the light blue Peanut dark blue? (See Retired Peanut.) Actually, Righty is a scarce vari—n of Peanut who is still relatively affordable and highly recommende— most collectors, a $5 plush elephant (even one without tusks) is —ish. Strange elephant facts: Elephants sleep standing up, —, frightened, and wave their ears to show aggressiveness. Th— jokes.

 78

✪ PINCHERS ✪
(The Lobster)

This lobster loves to pinch

Moving forward slow as a snail!

Eating his food inch by inch

Balancing carefully with his tail

ORIGINAL 9

 Birthday: June 19, 1993

TOTAL BORN:	6,000,000	Likely to be Retired: 1998	
Est. Survival (2008):	600,000	Style #4026	

ISSUE PRICE	**$5.00 - $7.00**
1998 Value	**$5.00 - $15.00**
Year 2008 (est.)	**$60.00**

 Recommended

BEANIE HUNTER TIPS: In order to collect all 9 "original" Beanie Babies with original tags, you do not have to spend $1,000 apiece for "Punchers" (the first version of Pinchers) or Brownie (the early Cubbie.) Pinchers and Cubbie were issued with the first generation heart-shaped tags and are valued at $40 - $50 each. The current Pinchers is usually fairly easy to find for $5 - $7. But don't wait until next year, or inflation may get a grip on the price of lobster. Remember: lobster is a delicacy.

PINKY

 ⟡ ⟡

(The Flamingo)

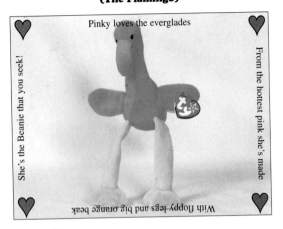

Pinky loves the everglades

She's the Beanie that you seek!

From the hottest pink she's made

With floppy legs and big orange beak

 Birthday: February 13, 1995

TOTAL BORN:	3,000,000	**Likely to be Retired: 1998**
Est. Survival (2008):	300,000	**Style #4072**

ISSUE PRICE	$5.00 - $7.00
1998 Value	$5.00 - $20.00
Year 2008 (est.)	$75.00

> 👍👍 **Highly Recommended**

BEANIE HUNTER TIPS: Where the heck have all the flamingos flown? Pinky is one of the scarcer "current" Beanies (and Teenie Beanies) and is worth tucking away in your secret aviary. Kids, did you know that Pinky is hiding a big white tooth below one of her wings? If you find it, put it under your pillow and you will receive a shiny new dime!

☼ **POUCH** ☼
(The Kangaroo)

My little pouch is handy I've found

Knowing my baby is safe and near.

It helps me carry my baby around

I hop up and down without any fear.

 Birthday: November 6, 1996

TOTAL BORN:	**2,000,000**	**Likely to be Retired: 1999**
Est. Survival (2008):	**200,000**	**Style #4161**

ISSUE PRICE	**$5.00 - $7.00**
1998 Value	**$5.00 - $7.00**
Year 2008 (est.)	**$85.00**

 Highly Recommended

BEANIE HUNTER TIPS: Many Beanie observers (including us) have speculated that this unique "Beanie Mom" (and child) will be retired shortly. (If so, look for Punch the boy kangaroo.) One reason why Pouch may exit stage left is that her "baby" turns out to be nothing more than a plush head on a string! Yuk! No way is Ty going to give us two full Beanies for the price of one.

☼ POUNCE ☼

(The Brown Cat)

Sneaking and slinking down the hall

NEW FOR '98

Through the rooms and down the stairs!

To pounce upon a fluffy yarn of ball

Under the table, around the chairs

Birthday: August 28, 1997

TOTAL BORN:	250,000	Likely to be Retired:	2000
Est. Survival (2008):	25,000	Style #:	None

ISSUE PRICE	$5.00 - $7.00
1998 Value	$5.00 - $7.00
Year 2008 (est.)	$60.00

Highly Recommended

BEANIE HUNTER TIPS: The white-pawed Pounce has a tendency to be overly rambunctious when meeting new friends. She quickly warms up to the first person who adopts her, but it's up to you to make sure visitors don't get pounced on. This fancy feline likes to be petted very, very gently, or watch out!

☼ **PRANCE** ☼
(The Tabby Cat)

She darts around and swats the air

NEW FOR '98

Listen closely and you'll hear her purr!

Then looks confused when nothing's there

Pick her up and pet her soft fur

 Birthday: November 20, 1997

TOTAL BORN:	250,000	**Likely to be Retired: 2000**	
Est. Survival (2008):	25,000	**Style #: None**	

ISSUE PRICE	**$5.00 - $7.00**
1998 Value	**$5.00 - $12.00**
Year 2008 (est.)	**$60.00**

 Highly Recommended

BEANIE HUNTER TIPS: Although Ty forgot to place the signature "M" on Prance's forehead, this terrific tabby is a spirited addition to the Beanie Baby cat family. (She's like a junior Stripes with blue eyes.) If there's one thing about Prance we really like, it's how ticklish she is. Please wear gloves when tickling her under the arms, as Prance's baby teeth are still razor sharp.

☼ **PRINCESS** ☼
(Commemorative Purple Bear With White Heart)

Like an angel, she came from heaven above

The world to share, to give, to reach

She shared her compassion, her pain, her love

She only stayed with us long enough to reach

👑 **Birthday: December 1, 1997** (Not shown on 1997 tags)

TOTAL BORN: 60,000*   Likely to be Retired: 1998
Est. Survival (2008): 6,000   **Style #** (None on 1997 toys)

ISSUE PRICE	**$5.00 - $7.00**
1998 Value	**$5.00 - $250.00**
Year 2008 (est.)	**$600.00**

👍👍 **Highly Recommended**

BEANIE HUNTER TIPS: Behaving more like a scarce "limited edition" (or an heirloom) than a normal Beanie Baby, this beautiful tribute to Princess Diana actually changed hands at $250 to $500 December, 1997. As we are not privy to Ty's 1998 plans, we assume that this Beanie's history as a collectible will parallel Peace (rather than the colored Teddies) unless there turns out to be a rare variety. Highly possible! Hope you can afford this treasured Princess soon! (*NOTE: December, 1997 production figures only based on a limit of 12 per store.)

84

☼ PUFFER ☼
(The Puffin)

What in the world does a puffin do?

NEW FOR '98

Before she answered, she flew away!

We're sure that you would like to know too

We asked Puffer how she spends her days

 Birthday: November 3, 1997

TOTAL BORN:	250,000	Likely to be Retired:	2000
Est. Survival (2008):	25,000	Style #:	None

ISSUE PRICE	$5.00 - $7.00
1998 Value	$5.00 - $12.00
Year 2008 (est.)	$60.00

 Highly Recommended

BEANIE HUNTER TIPS: Contrary to popular belief, the "Chicago" puffin evolved in the state of Illinois and is a direct descendant of Peter Piper (the purple puffin who pecked a pail of pickled peanuts.) Sporting similar colors and the physique of Waddle the Penguin, "Puffer" does not like to be in the company of cigar smoking walruses.

☼ **PUGSLEY** ☼
(The Pug)

Pugsly is picky about what he will wear

Until he noticed his wrinkled coat!

Never a spot, a stain or a tear

Image is something of which he'll gloat

 Birthday: May 2, 1996

TOTAL BORN:	1,000,000	Likely to be Retired: 1999
Est. Survival (2008):	100,000	Style #4106

ISSUE PRICE	**$5.00 - $7.00**
1998 Value	**$5.00 - $7.00**
Year 2008 (est.)	**$60.00**

 Recommended

BEANIE HUNTER TIPS: There are a lot of cute pugs around (real and plush), but there is only one Pugsley! A pug dog has trouble breathing through his small, compressed snout. If you notice Pugsley gasping for air in your living room, rush him outside for a heavy dose of fresh oxygen. Despite his handicap, Pugsley will remain a Beanie favorite until Lassie comes home!

✿ **QUACKERS** ✿
(The Duck)

There is a duck by the name of Quackers

But he'll come to the shore to be with you!

Every night he eats animal crackers

He swims in a lake that's clear and blue

 Birthday: April 19, 1994

TOTAL BORN: 5,000,000	**Likely to be Retired: 2000**
Est. Survival (2008): 500,000	**Style #4024**

ISSUE PRICE	**$5.00 - $7.00**
1998 Value	**$5.00 - $7.00**
Year 2008 (est.)	**$60.00**

👍 Recommended

BEANIE HUNTER TIPS: Quack! Quack! Quack! means "We love Quackers!" Quackers has been made even more famous by being included in one of Les & Sue Fox's Beanie Baby songs: "Spot Without A Spot." In this song, a child laments his futile desire to own the rare Beanies, such as "Quackers Without Wings." (See Retired.) Some ducks mate for life, just as some Beanie collectors will never divorce their precious toys. Contrary to popular belief, Quackers is not one of the original 9 Beanie Babies.

☼ **RAINBOW** ☼
(The Chameleon)

Red, green, blue and yellow

NEW FOR '98

Rainbow was made especially for you!

This chameleon is a colorful fellow

A blend of colors, his own unique hue

🎂 **Birthday: October 14, 1997**

TOTAL BORN:	250,000	**Likely to be Retired: 1999**
Est. Survival (2008):	25,000	**Style #: None**

ISSUE PRICE	**$5.00 - $7.00**
1998 Value	**$5.00 - $12.00**
Year 2008 (est.)	**$100.00**

 Highly Recommended

BEANIE HUNTER TIPS: Perhaps the strangest of the new 1998 releases (actually announced 12/31/97), Rainbow the Chameleon loves to camouflage himself when the sun comes up. Don't panic if you find Peanut the Dark Blue elephant in your Beanie Collection one morning and then he's gone after lunch. It's only Rainbow, proving that Beanie Babies can do whatever they want. (NOTE: Rainbow and Iggy's tags were reversed in January, 1998.)

RINGO
(The Raccoon)

Ringo hides behind his mask

Just about anything, it doesn't matter!

He will come out, if you should ask

He loves to chitter. He loves to chatter.

 Birthday: July 14, 1995

TOTAL BORN: 3,000,000   Likely to be Retired: 2000
Est. Survival (2008):   300,000   Style #4014

ISSUE PRICE	**$5.00 - $7.00**
1998 Value	**$5.00 - $7.00**
Year 2008 (est.)	**$60.00**

> 👍 Recommended

BEANIE HUNTER TIPS: As you may have observed, raccoons are "omnivorous" animals (they eat everything.) No matter how tightly you fasten down the lid of your garbage can, these clever and persistent critters will find a way to spread your banana peels and left-over meatloaf all over the neighborhood. Ringo the Beanie Baby raccoon is the pleasant exception, exhibiting only the best qualities of the breed. A scarcer variety of Ringo was made in the correct greyish brown shade of the true-life masked marauder.

☼ **ROARY** ☼
(The Lion)

Deep in the jungle they crowned him king

He hears his roar and runs away!

But being brave is not his thing

A cowardly lion some say say

 Birthday: February 20, 1996

TOTAL BORN:	**1,000,000**	**Likely to be Retired: 2000**
Est. Survival (2008):	**100,000**	**Style #4069**

ISSUE PRICE	**$5.00 - $7.00**
1998 Value	**$5.00 - $12.00**
Year 2008 (est.)	**$85.00**

Highly Recommended

BEANIE HUNTER TIPS: Roary is the "pride" of the Beanie Babies! In fact, if you think Roary is really cute, you ain't lion! His majestic mane makes him a stand-out in any plush crowd, although Roary gets along very nicely with the domestic dogs and cats. As time goes on, you may find it more difficult to track down a perfect specimen, so hunt for a spare or two. Remember, it's a jungle out there. (Question: Does Roary deserve a lioness pal?)

☼ **ROVER** ☼
(The Red Dog)

♥ This dog is red and his name is Rover ♥

But worry not, he won't bite!

If you call him he is sure to come over

He barks and plays with all his might!

 Birthday: May 30, 1996

TOTAL BORN: 2,000,000	Likely to be Retired: 1998
Est. Survival (2008): 200,000	Style #4101

ISSUE PRICE	**$5.00 - $7.00**
1998 Value	**$5.00 - $15.00**
Year 2008 (est.)	**$75.00**

 Highly Recommended

BEANIE HUNTER TIPS: If you've been postponing making a major investment in Rover (hey, $5 - $7 doesn't grow on trees), you'll turn red if Rover is suddenly retired. For Beanie dog lovers who think Rover is just a crimson Bones, check out Rover's fluffy tail, thin forehead and lack of eyebrows. Although both pups wear heart-shaped dog tags, only Rover is specially trained to stop when the light turns red. A special Rover candy promotion was licensed by Ty to Fanny Farmer in late 1997.

SCOOP

(The Pelican)

All day long he scoops up fish

Hoping those fish are very slow!

To fill his bill, his wish

Diving fast and diving low

 Birthday: July 1, 1996

TOTAL BORN: 2,000,000	Likely to be Retired: 1998
Est. Survival (2008): 200,000	Style #4107

ISSUE PRICE	**$5.00 - $7.00**
1998 Value	**$5.00 - $15.00**
Year 2008 (est.)	**$75.00**

Highly
Recommended

BEANIE HUNTER TIPS: Last year we mentioned that Scoop's bill contains plush sardines. Actually, we were just kidding. It's filled with "Goldie" Teenie Beanies! Scoop the Pelican is a typical, fun-loving, dive bombing aquatic bird. He has been known to sit quietly on a towel rack in a kid's bathroom for hours, and then without warning to crash into a bath tub in search of a big toe. It is best to wear rubber boots when Scoop is keeping an eye on you.

✧ SCOTTIE ✧
(The Black Terrier)

Scottie is a friendly sort

His best best friends are you and me!

Even though his legs are short

He is always happy as can be

🎂 **Birthday: June 15, 1996**

TOTAL BORN: 2,000,000
Est. Survival (2008):   200,000

Likely to be Retired: 2000

Style #4102

ISSUE PRICE	**$5.00 - $7.00**
1998 Value	**$5.00 - $7.00**
Year 2008 (est.)	**$60.00**

👍 Recommended

BEANIE HUNTER TIPS: As of early 1998, Scottie, Fleece, Curly and Tuffy represent the nappy-furred Beanie Babies. Some readers noticed a black terrier on page 5 of last year's edition. That's our dog, Lance, the Kerry Blue Terrier (the national dog of Ireland), who takes no offense at being compared to the shorter, more nippy Scotsman. Scottie the black terrier has not been this famous since the 1940's, when President Franklin D. Roosevelt often appeared in public with his pet Scottie, Fala.

☼ **SEAWEED** ☼
(The Otter)

Seaweed is what she likes to eat

If you haven't, maybe you "otter"!

It's supposed to be a delicious treat

Have you tried a treat from the water

🎂 **Birthday: March 19, 1996**

TOTAL BORN: 2,000,000	Likely to be Retired: 2000
Est. Survival (2008): 200,000	Style #4080

ISSUE PRICE	**$5.00 - $7.00**
1998 Value	**$5.00 - $7.00**
Year 2008 (est.)	**$60.00**

 Recommended

BEANIE HUNTER TIPS: Seaweed is into health food. Not only does he enjoy highly nutritional seaweed raw, but he likes it in the form of cookies (fruit juice sweetened), pasta and home-baked bread. Like his busy pal, Bucky, Seaweed is an aquatic mammal who likes to eat, swim and lounge around on his back. Seaweed also loves to be patted on his soft, wrinkly belly. (NOTE: Otters can break open nuts on their chests.)

SLY
(The Fox)

Sly is a fox and tricky is he

He'll peek out from his den!

Please don't chase him, let him be

If you want him, just say when

 Birthday: September 12, 1996

TOTAL BORN: 2,000,000	**Likely to be Retired: 2000**
Est. Survival (2008): 200,000	**Style #4115**

ISSUE PRICE	**$5.00 - $7.00**
1998 Value	**$5.00 - $7.00**
Year 2008 (est.)	**$60.00**

👍 Recommended

BEANIE HUNTER TIPS: Sly the Fox (no relation to authors) is a perennial food hunter. (Note his roguish smile.) The dictionary defines "sly" as: "crafty and cunning." This not only applies to a foxy Beanie, but to the Beanie hunters who adore him. Kids are calling for "Ice the Arctic Fox," a Les and Sue Fox concept. (See also retired Sly.)

☼ **SMOOCHY** ☼
(The Frog)

Is he a frog or maybe a prince?

Be the one to give him a kiss!

This confusion makes him wince

Find the answer, help him with this

 Birthday: October 1, 1997

TOTAL BORN:	250,000	Likely to be Retired:	2000
Est. Survival (2008):	25,000	Style #:	None

ISSUE PRICE	**$5.00 - $7.00**
1998 Value	**$5.00 - $12.00**
Year 2008 (est.)	**$60.00**

Highly Recommended

BEANIE HUNTER TIPS: Leave it to Ty to surprise and delight frog lovers everywhere! Last year (before he retired) we mentioned that a single kiss could turn Legs into a handsome prince. Welcome Smoochy, the new bulging-eyed frog prince of Beanie Babies. (Caution: The authors of this book cannot be responsible for what happens if Legs and Smoochy's lips touch. Do so at your own risk!)

SNIP

(The Siamese Cat)

Snip the cat is Siamese

Playing with you is her favorite thing!

She'll be your friend if you please

So toss her a toy or a piece of string

 Birthday: October 22, 1996

TOTAL BORN: 3,000,000	**Likely to be Retired: 2000**
Est. Survival (2008): 300,000	**Style #4120**

ISSUE PRICE	$5.00 - $7.00
1998 Value	$5.00 - $7.00
Year 2008 (est.)	$60.00

 Recommended

BEANIE HUNTER TIPS: What rhymes with Nip, Zip, Chip and the blue-eyed Flip and Snip? (How about Slip, Dip, Hip, Whip and Rip?) Seriously, there is no better place to start your Beanie collection than with the domestic cats, then slinking ahead to the larger beasts. At present, Beanie dog pets out-number the felines, but look for multiple births in 1998 and 1999. (All of the present kitties will be replaced within 3 years.) As there are more than 100 varieties of cats (originally tamed in Egypt), Ty has plenty of rhyming options. (Skip?)

SNORT
(The Bull)

Although Snort is not so tall

Can you guess his favorite team?

He loves to play basketball

He is a star player in his dreams

Birthday: May 15, 1995

TOTAL BORN: 2,000,000
Est. Survival (2008): 200,000

Likely to be Retired: 2001
Style #4002

ISSUE PRICE	$5.00 - $7.00
1998 Value	$5.00 - $7.00
Year 2008 (est.)	$75.00

 Recommended

BEANIE HUNTER TIPS: In our opinion, Snort is actually an improved version of the rarer Tabasco. (See Retired). However, due to the continuing demand for Tabasco, many collectors ignore Snort. (This makes him see red, so stand back!) Snort recently told us he misses Bessie the cow and hopes Daisy won't be retired in 1998. (Tough luck, buddy!)

 98

SPIKE
(The Rhinoceros)

Spike the rhino likes to stampede

You can be his friend if you like!

He's the bruiser that you need

Gentle to birds on his back and spike

 Birthday: August 13, 1996

TOTAL BORN:	2,000,000	**Likely to be Retired:**	2000
Est. Survival (2008):	200,000	**Style #4060**	

ISSUE PRICE	$5.00 - $7.00
1998 Value	$5.00 - $7.00
Year 2008 (est.)	$75.00

Highly
Recommended

BEANIE HUNTER TIPS: Sharing the same fabric as Tank (retired) and Mel, Spike the Rhino may soon become an endangered Beanie as well as an endangered species. (We hate rhino poachers!) If you are ever confronted by a rogue rhinoceros, stand still (Rhinos can't see well. A man and a tree trunk look the same to him) but don't hiccup. This jungle beast has a keen sense of smell and hearing.

☼ **SPINNER** ☼
(The Spider)

Does this spider make you scared?

In fact, this spider really likes you!

Among many people that feeling is shared

Remember spiders have feelings too

 Birthday: October 28, 1996

TOTAL BORN: 500,000   Likely to be Retired: 2000
Est. Survival (2008): 50,000   Style #4036

ISSUE PRICE	$5.00 - $7.00
1998 Value	$5.00 - $25.00
Year 2008 (est.)	$150.00

 Highly Recommended

BEANIE HUNTER TIPS: Another recent release that is hard to find and may cost you 5 times its suggested retail price. Like Web (retired), Spinner is a wonderfully cute (and scary) insect. He differs from Web in that his eyes are red thread, his belly is black, his legs are skinnier and his back is made of the same fabric as Stripes. Spinner certainly fills the gap left by Web's sudden retirement in 1995. Now all you have to do is find one!

 100

☼ **SPUNKY** ☼
(The Cocker Spaniel)

Bouncing around without much grace

He'll run so fast he'll trip over his ears!

To jump on your lap and lick your face

But watch him closely, he has no fears

 Birthday: January 14, 1997

TOTAL BORN:	250,000	**Likely to be Retired: 1999**
Est. Survival (2008):	25,000	**Style #: None**

ISSUE PRICE	$5.00 - $7.00
1998 Value	$5.00 - $25.00
Year 2008 (est.)	$75.00

 Highly Recommended

BEANIE HUNTER TIPS: Cocker Spaniel lovers gave Spunky a standing ovation when he made his debut on New Year's Eve! Did you know there are 400 distinct breeds and varieties, according to Fogle's "Encyclopedia of the Dog"? And who do we find on page 202? You guessed it! Spunky's father, whose ancestors, (according to Fogle) "arrived in the United States in 1670 on The Mayflower" (No kidding - Look it up!)

☼ SQUEALER ☼
(The Pig)

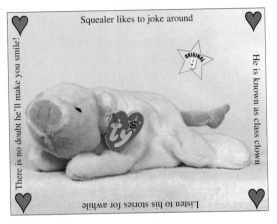

Squealer likes to joke around

There is no doubt he'll make you smile!

He is known as class clown

Listen to his stories for awhile

ORIGINAL

 Birthday: April 23, 1993

TOTAL BORN:	5,000,000	**Likely to be Retired: 1998**
Est. Survival (2008):	500,000	**Style #4005**

ISSUE PRICE	$5.00 - $7.00
1998 Value	$5.00 - $7.00
Year 2008 (est.)	$60.00

 Recommended

BEANIE HUNTER TIPS: Another original Beanie Baby worth searching for with the first generation hang tag ($40 - $50). Last year we referred to Squealer as a "he." Well... Ex-cuuuuse us! This delicate pink piggy is obviously of the female persuasion (a "sow.") In fact, it is rumored that Squealer may be bearing a pair of new piglets soon: "Wheeler" and "Dealer." No wonder this prime porker has been consuming twice the average amount of water most pigs drink, 2-1/2 gallons a day.

☼ STINKY ☼
(The Skunk)

Deep in the woods he lived in a cave

Hoping one day he wouldn't stink!

Perfume and mints were the gifts he gave

He showered every night in the kitchen sink

🎂 **Birthday: February 13, 1995**

TOTAL BORN: 3,000,000   Likely to be Retired: 1999
Est. Survival (2008): 300,000   Style #4017

ISSUE PRICE	**$5.00 - $7.00**
1998 Value	**$5.00 - $7.00**
Year 2008 (est.)	**$60.00**

 Recommended

BEANIE HUNTER TIPS: Now in his third year as a Beanie Baby, Stinky the Skunk has begun to socialize with Ringo, Nuts and other back yard dwellers. Of course, when the boys go out on the town, Stinky always wears his favorite scent: Brut. (He used to like English Leather, but it left a faint yellow stain along his white streak.)

☼ STRETCH ☼
(The Ostrich)

She thinks when her head is underground

To play hide and seek with this bird!

The rest of her body can't be found

The Beanie Babies think it's absurd

 Birthday: September 21, 1997

TOTAL BORN:	250,000	Likely to be Retired: 2000
Est. Survival (2008):	25,000	Style #: None

ISSUE PRICE	$5.00 - $7.00
1998 Value	$5.00 - $12.00
Year 2008 (est.)	$60.00

 Highly Recommended

BEANIE HUNTER TIPS: Okay, Ty, you got us again! Although we still believe Pinky will be retired this year, now there are two long-legged big birds to feast your eyes on. Last year we predicted "Kick" the Ostrich and this year "Stretch" the Ferret. Put 'em together and whadaya get? Bibbity-Bobbity-Beanie! (Careful, don't trip over that big egg we laid!)

☼ **STRIPES** ☼
(The Tiger)

Stripes was never fierce nor strong

So he came to his friends at Ty!

So with tigers, he didn't get along

Jungle life was hard to get by

Birthday: June 11, 1995

TOTAL BORN:	5,000,000	**Likely to be Retired: 2000**
Est. Survival (2008):	500,000	**Style #4065**

ISSUE PRICE	**$5.00 - $7.00**
1998 Value	**$5.00 - $7.00**
Year 2008 (est.)	**$60.00**

 Recommended

BEANIE HUNTER TIPS: Contrary to popular belief, the brawny orange and black tiger is indigenous to Asia, not Africa. Outside of Asia, only the rare white tiger resides in the Rewa Forest of India. Technically, the original dark stripes (See Retired) is the more accurate color of the largest jungle cat. (Praytell why Spinner the Spider is now wearing Stripes' old coat?) We've moved up Stripes' expected retirement by two years. He (and Blizzard) may be extinct even sooner.

☼ TUFFY ☼
(The Terrier)

Taking off with a thunderous blast

He never took off his training wheels!

Tuffy rides his motorcycle fast

The Beanies roll with laughs & squeals

 Birthday: October 12, 1996

TOTAL BORN: 1,000,000
Est. Survival (2008): 100,000

Likely to be Retired: 1999
Style #4108

ISSUE PRICE	**$5.00 - $7.00**
1998 Value	**$5.00 - $7.00**
Year 2008 (est.)	**$60.00**

 Recommended

BEANIE HUNTER TIPS: The newest of the nappy-coated Beanies (see also Scottie, Fleece and Curly), the compact, brown and tan Tuffy is too small to be an Airedale so he must be a Welsh terrier. As terrier experts (we've lived with them since 1968), we should warn you that Tuffy will not back down from a fight. Don't be misled by his cute, tipped ears. Tuffy is genuinely tough! Pairing him with Scottie is not a bad idea, but be prepared to referee. Separate doghouses are recommended.

✿ TWIGS ✿
(The Giraffe)

Twigs has his head in the clouds

What an unusual friend he will make!

He stands tall, he stands proud

With legs so skinny they wobble and shake

🎂 Birthday: May 19, 1995

TOTAL BORN:	4,000,000	Likely to be Retired: 1998
Est. Survival (2008):	400,000	Style #4068

ISSUE PRICE	$5.00 - $7.00
1998 Value	$5.00 - $15.00
Year 2008 (est.)	$60.00

 Recommended

BEANIE HUNTER TIPS: Strange and amazing fact about the 18-foot giraffe, world's tallest animal: When a baby giraffe is born, it falls almost 6 feet to the ground! (Giraffes give birth standing up.) One of the few animals with color vision, the Americanized Twigs misses the beautiful foliage and reddish-blue sunsets of central and southern Africa. If you sing him our new Beanie Baby song, "Congo and Bongo," he will get very melancholy.

☼ VALENTINO ☼
(White Teddy Bear with Red Heart)

His heart is red and full of love

Feel the love he has for you!

He cares for you so give him a hug

Keep him close when feeling blue

🎂 Birthday: February 14, 1994

TOTAL BORN: 1,000,000
Est. Survival (2008): 100,000

Likely to be Retired: 1998
Style #4058

ISSUE PRICE	$5.00 - $7.00
1998 Value	$5.00 - $25.00
Year 2008 (est.)	$125.00

 Highly Recommended

BEANIE HUNTER TIPS: Issued for Valentine's Day, Valentino is much scarcer than commonly believed. Along with Britannia, Curly and Princess, he is the oldest of the four current Beanie bears. We suspect Valentino is manufactured for February and turns up here and there during the rest of the year. If you give a loved one Godiva chocolates and Valentino, remind the recipient to lick his or her fingertips before touching white plush. In years to come, a perfect Valentino could be as hard to find as true love.

✺ WADDLE ✺
(The Penguin)

Waddle the Penguin likes to dress up

He always trips over his tails!

Every night he wears his tux

When Waddle walks, it never fails

 Birthday: December 19, 1995

TOTAL BORN:	3,000,000	Likely to be Retired: 1999
Est. Survival (2008):	300,000	Style #4075

ISSUE PRICE	**$5.00 - $7.00**
1998 Value	**$5.00 - $7.00**
Year 2008 (est.)	**$60.00**

👍 Recommended

BEANIE HUNTER TIPS: This waddling Beanie was originally born in the South Pole (Antarctica) where 20 playful varieties of penguins reside. The ice-skating champion of the Beanie crowd, Waddle has surprisingly good balance. If you drop him on the floor, he almost always lands on his beans. Better wing it to the store to snatch up a pair or two of this neat little guy before next winter.

WAVES
(The Whale)

Join him today on the Internet

Our web page is his home turf!

Don't be afraid to get your feet wet

He taught all the Beanies how to surf

Birthday: December 8, 1996

TOTAL BORN: 1,000,000	**Likely to be Retired:** 2000
Est. Survival (2008): 100,000	**Style #4084**

ISSUE PRICE	**$5.00 - $7.00**
1998 Value	**$5.00 - $7.00**
Year 2008 (est.)	**$60.00**

 Recommended

BEANIE HUNTER TIPS: Yes, we know all about Waves' mixed-up tags! (see "Echo") Relatively minor modifications distinguish the black and white Waves from his predecessor the black and white Splash. Both "killer" whales are realistic looking specimens lacking only their characteristic white markings behind the eyes. Did you know Orca whales can be up to thirty feet long? We've heard that Ty is adding a new plush line next year: Actual size animals for only $5!

☼ **WEENIE** ☼
(The Dachshund)

Weenie the dog is quite a sight

And considers himself to be top dog!

Long of body and short of height

He perches himself high on a log

 Birthday: July 20, 1995

TOTAL BORN:	2,000,000	**Likely to be Retired:** 2000
Est. Survival (2008):	200,000	**Style #4013**

ISSUE PRICE	$5.00 - $7.00
1998 Value	$5.00 - $7.00
Year 2008 (est.)	$60.00

 Recommended

BEANIE HUNTER TIPS: The short-legged big-eared Weenie is a prize addition to your Beanie dog collection. Since he could be retired at any time (like all the other canines), we recommend not waiting too long to rescue a Weenie from the dog pound. Just look at those soulful, compelling eyes. If you can resist Weenie, you are one tough cookie, er, dog biscuit.

☼ WRINKLES ☼
(The Bulldog)

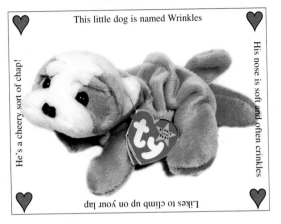

This little dog is named Wrinkles

He's a cheery sort of chap!

His nose is soft and often crinkles

Likes to climb up on your lap

 Birthday: May 1, 1996

TOTAL BORN: 2,000,000	**Likely to be Retired: 1998**
Est. Survival (2008): 200,000	**Style #4103**

ISSUE PRICE	**$5.00 - $7.00**
1998 Value	**$5.00 - $7.00**
Year 2008 (est.)	**$60.00**

 Recommended

BEANIE HUNTER TIPS: Wrinkles the Beanie Baby is all dog, and that's no bull! If you love Wrinkles (who doesn't?), you might want to purchase him in the two larger sizes of Ty's other plush toys. ("Big Wrinkles" is named "Winston.") Wrinkles is covered with a generous amount of fabric. In fact, every once in a while, it is reported that some long lost Teenie Beanies fall out of his folds.

ZIGGY

☼ ☼

(The Zebra)

Ziggy likes soccer – he's a referee

But Ziggy the Zebra doesn't care!

That way he watches the games for free

The other Beanies don't think it's fair

🎂 **Birthday: December 24, 1995**

TOTAL BORN: 5,000,000	Likely to be Retired: 2000
Est. Survival (2008): 500,000	Style #4063

ISSUE PRICE	$5.00 - $7.00
1998 Value	$5.00 - $7.00
Year 2008 (est.)	$60.00

 Recommended

BEANIE HUNTER TIPS: Sporting a different stripe pattern than Blizzard the White Tiger, Ziggy the Zebra is styled in the mode of Derby the Horse and Mystic the Unicorn. Of these three figures, only Ziggy was never made with a fine yarn mane and tail (to our knowledge.) According to unreliable sources, Ziggy, Derby and Mystic are actually half brothers (through marriage), but a search of court records has revealed that they are only kissing cousins. (NOTE: Recently, Ziggy has appeared with a "swelled" head.)

ZIP

(The Black Cat)

Keep Zip by your side all the day through

Zip will always believe in you!

Zip is good luck, you'll see it's true

When you have something you need to do

 Birthday: March 28, 1994

TOTAL BORN:	4,000,000	Likely to be Retired: 1998
Est. Survival (2008):	400,000	Style #4004

ISSUE PRICE	$5.00 - $7.00
1998 Value	$5.00 - $15.00
Year 2008 (est.)	$60.00

 Recommended

BEANIE HUNTER TIPS: Like Nip, the Zip pictured above is known as "Version 3." (See Retired section for types 1 & 2.) It is rather confusing to remember all of the subtle differences between the three Zips (and the three Nips.) In fact, Milton-Bradley has been developing an exciting new board game entitled: Nip-Zip-Opoly.

Beanie Baby
Rags-To-Riches Quiz

Which native son of Illinois grew up to change America?

Hint: He wasn't born in a log cabin. (His new office building, above, isn't a log cabin either!)

BEANIE BABY MARKET UPDATE

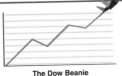

The Dow Beanie

Retired Beanie Babies

HOT! HOT! HOT!

14 HOTTEST RETIRED BEANIES

Retired Beanie	Highest Trade	Retired Beanie	Highest Trade
Bumble	$600	Quacker	$2,000
Flutter	900	Peking/Chilly	1,800
Garcia	175	Rex	750
Humphrey	1,750	Righty	300
Lefty	300	Spot (No Spot)	2,000
Libearty	375	Teddies (Rare)	2,000
Peanut (Dark)	4,500	Web	1,200

February, 1998 - Wouldn't you know it? Just as we were going to press, the retired Beanie Baby market went crazy! Fueled by "TV Shopping" promotions (plus genuine supply/demand), The Dow Beanie has flown off the charts! Is this temporary or the next move toward our "optimistic" 10-year price predictions? As suggested throughout our book, retired Beanie Babies are very volatile! (For most collectors, these toys are already way out of reach.) How high will wealthy buyers drive prices in 1998? Will prices drop back? Let's wait and see!

MORE BEANIE NEWS: In addition to reversed tags, Iggy and Rainbow are not anatomically correct! In real life, an Iguana has a jagged ridge along its spine, and a Chameleon has a thick neck collar. It is also rumored that due to royal licensing requirements, Ty, Inc. may be discontinuing the production of the Princess Beanie Baby.

The Beanie Baby
Collection

of

Les, Sue and Jamie Fox

The "Retired" Beanies
Introduction

This section of The Beanie Baby Handbook contains the 99 Beanie Babies "retired" by Ty, Inc.

Each page provides the same general information as the "Current" Beanies. (See Introduction to previous section for details.) In addition, these pages include the actual date that a retired Beanie Baby was taken out of production by Ty, Inc. Starting January 1, 1997, such dates correspond to official announcements on the Ty.com web site. Between 1993 and mid-1996, there were no official retirement dates. Therefore, we have relied on the most accurate information available, and some of our retirement dates may be off by a month. This minor lack of precision is not critical to collecting retired Beanie Babies.

Retired Beanie Babies vary in scarcity and value. Some of the extremely rare Beanies, such as Peanut the Dark Blue Elephant, are appropriate for serious collectors only. (Unless, of course, you were lucky enough to find one for $5.) In fact, other than toys priced at $25 to perhaps $250, new collectors should really take their time deciding which toys to collect and how much to spend. As you can see, some of today's retired Beanies are not cheap! If this hobby continues to grow, as we believe it will, 10 years from now even today's "shocking" high prices may seem low. After all, people were shocked when Picasso's paintings surpassed the million-dollar mark. Recently, one sold for $25 million!

However, it is a good idea to study the market, and not be enticed by the possibility of "making a killing" in Beanie Babies. As a good friend once told us, it is always easier to buy than to sell. So our best advice to even serious Beanie Baby collectors is to live within your means (if you're rich, go ahead and spring for that Dark Blue Peanut - in fact, buy a matched pair!) and to collect primarily for the sheer joy of collecting. Remember, if you buy something because you love it, you will never be disappointed. (Example: "Abner" the greatest American Folk Art Rooster, pictured on back cover, circa 1920.) But if you buy to make money, anything can happen.

As we go to press, the most popular retired Beanies continue to be the 12 Teddy Bears (far outperforming world class Steiff bears!), the 3 Dinosaurs (apparently, wealthy parents are not extinct), Lefty and Righty, and selected rarities such as Slither the Snake, Peking the Panda and Humphrey the Camel. Among these toys, Lefty and Righty are the most affordable and probably the safest to collect in terms of value. Incidentally, prices are based on surveys among reputable Beanie Baby specialists (know and trust your dealer) and are highly volatile. If the Beanie market remains "hot", by mid-1998 add 10% of the estimated 2008 value to this year's prices. (Example: Add $150 to Lefty = $300!)

ALLY
(The Alligator)

RETIRED
Sept., 1997

When Ally gets out of classes

He's the coolest gator in the land!

He wears a hat and dark glasses

He plays bass in a street band

Birthday: March 14, 1994

TOTAL BORN:	3,000,000	**Style #4032**
Est. Survival (2008):	300,000	

ISSUE PRICE	**$5.00**
1998 Value	**$30.00**
Year 2008 (est.)	**$150.00**

 Recommended

Reduce values up to 50%
unless mint condition / mint tag.

BEANIE HUNTER TIPS: Amazing alligator tales: An alligator can grow to be 23 feet long and live for more than 100 years. Last year, before Ally's premature retirement (we predicted 1998), we believed our toothy pal would be worth $40 in 10 years. Now that he's jumped from $5 to $30 in one short year (proving alligators can jump pretty far), his true future has emerged from below the surface.

Sept., 1997

☼ BESSIE ☼
(The Brown & White Cow)

Bessie the cow likes to dance and sing

She'll sing you a song to put you to sleep!

Because music is her favorite thing

Every night when you are counting sheep

Birthday: June 27, 1995

TOTAL BORN:	**2,000,000**	**Style #4009**
Est. Survival (2008):	**200,000**	

ISSUE PRICE	**$5.00**
1998 Value	**$35.00**
Year 2008 (est.)	**$175.00**

 Recommended

Reduce values up to 50%
unless mint condition / mint tag.

BEANIE HUNTER TIPS: Once again, this Beanie Baby has been retired before we expected (1999), making Bessie an instant success. Twice as scarce as Daisy, it now looks like Bessie's value could moo-ove even higher. With such cute pink mini-horns, this captivating cow could be tough to collect, so let's follow her to greener pastures.

 120

☼ **BRONTY** ☼
(The Brontosaurus)

RETIRED

June, 1996

 Birthday: 1995

TOTAL BORN:	100,000	**Style #4085**
Est. Survival (2008):	10,000	

ISSUE PRICE	**$5.00**
1998 Value	**$550.00**
Year 2008 (est.)	**$2,000.00**

 Highly Recommended

Reduce values up to 50%
unless mint condition / mint tag.

BEANIE HUNTER TIPS: In perfect condition, Bronty is still considered the rarest of the three dinosaurs, but Rex and Steg share the same stomping ground. Along with 10 million kids, we're hoping to see some fresh tonnage on the prehistoric horizon in 1998. Of course, the original giant lizards will always hold a place in our hearts... as long as they don't step on our superior vena cavas.

 121

☼ BROWNIE ☼
(The Brown Bear)

🎂 **Birthday: 1993**

TOTAL BORN:	1,000	Style #4010
Est. Survival (2008):	100	

ISSUE PRICE	**$5.00**
1998 Value	**$1,200.00**
Year 2008 (est.)	**$5,000.00**

 Highly Recommended

Reduce values up to 50% unless mint condition / mint tag.

BEANIE HUNTER TIPS: While he may never be considered the "king" of the Beanie Babies, some experts regard Brownie (and Punchers) as a rare prototype. There are subtle differences between the texture of Brownie's plush, his color and how his parts were sewn together compared to later Cubbies. For this reason, many collectors would like to own a first generation Cubbie. (Add our names to the list.)

☼ **BUBBLES** ☼
(The Fish)

RETIRED
May, 1997

All day long Bubbles likes to swim

Now she is ready to come home with you!

She never gets tired of flapping her fins

Bubbles lived in a sea of blue

 Birthday: July 2, 1995

TOTAL BORN: 1,000,000
Est. Survival (2008): 100,000

Style #4078

ISSUE PRICE	**$5.00**
1998 Value	**$50.00**
Year 2008 (est.)	**$200.00**

 Highly Recommended

Reduce values up to 50%
unless mint condition / mint tag.

BEANIE HUNTER TIPS: As we predicted, Bubbles was blown out of the water in 1997! Our strong recommendation to acquire Bubbles at up to $10 (when most collectors were reluctant to pay $5) turned out to be more than just a fish story. We still like Bubbles at $50, but one is probably enough. For a few dollars more, we're lured to Coral as an aquatic investment.

Dec., 1997

BUCKY

(The Beaver)

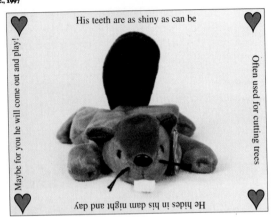

His teeth are as shiny as can be

Maybe for you he will come out and play!

Often used for cutting trees

He hides in his dam night and day

Birthday: June 8, 1995

TOTAL BORN:	3,000,000	**Style #4016**
Est. Survival (2008):	300,000	

ISSUE PRICE	**$5.00**
1998 Value	**$15.00**
Year 2008 (est.)	**$125.00**

Recommended	Reduce values up to 50% unless mint condition / mint tag.

BEANIE HUNTER TIPS: Originally from New York (Bucky is the state animal), did you know that Bucky's grandfather once advertised toothpaste on TV? Bucky is truly an exceptional beaver. He has a Ph."D." in engineering from the University of Notre Dam. Step back when Bucky is hard at work. He's clocked more than one observer with his paddle tail.

✿ **BUMBLE** ✿
(The Bee)

June, 1996

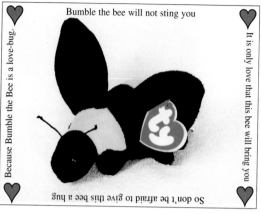

Bumble the bee will not sting you

Because Bumble the Bee is a love-bug.

It is only love that this bee will bring you

So don't be afraid to give this bee a hug.

 Birthday: 1995

TOTAL BORN:	75,000	Style #4045
Est. Survival (2008):	7,500	

ISSUE PRICE	**$5.00**
1998 Value	**$375.00**
Year 2008 (est.)	**$1,800.00**

 Highly
Recommended

Reduce values up to 50%
unless mint condition / mint tag.

BEANIE HUNTER TIPS: We've got the latest buzz on Bumble! First of all, now is the time to find and net yourself this rare and beautiful Queen Bee. If you wait until 1999, other collectors are going to swarm all over the small supply of mint condition Bumbles and you'll feel the sting. As a Beanie investment, Bumbles is truly a Triple-A rated Bee. (NOTE: Colors invisible to the human eye guide bees to the nectar of a flower.) Rare with a fourth generation Poem tag (value $425)

 125

CAW
(The Crow)

 Birthday: 1995

TOTAL BORN: 250,000
Est. Survival (2008): 25,000

Style #4071

ISSUE PRICE	**$5.00**
1998 Value	**$350.00**
Year 2008 (est.)	**$1,200.00**

 Highly Recommended

Reduce values up to 50% unless mint condition / mint tag.

BEANIE HUNTER TIPS: Increasingly difficult to find, Caw the Crow is another Beanie you should try to capture quickly. In our opinion, he's not as scarce as Bumble, nor does he offer quite as much long-range potential. However, the fact that his price has doubled in a year attests to his great popularity. (See last year's book for the poem we wrote for the poemless Caw.)

CHILLY
(The Polar Bear)

Dec., 1994

 Birthday: 1994

TOTAL BORN:	25,000	**Style #4012**
Est. Survival (2008):	2,500	

ISSUE PRICE	**$5.00**
1998 Value	**$1,000.00**
Year 2008 (est.)	**$3,500.00**

 Highly Recommended

Reduce values up to 50% unless mint condition / mint tag.

BEANIE HUNTER TIPS: Our research now shows Chilly to be twice as rare as we thought he was last year. NOTE: There is some confusion over when Chilly was manufactured and available from Ty. He was first pictured in the 1994 Ty catalog and still listed on Ty's 1995 wholesale price list, but we believe Chilly was actually made only in 1994. If you can find a perfect Chilly without a hang tag for half price, go for it!

CHOPS
(The Lamb)

Chops is a little lamb

This lamb is sure to go!

This lamb you'll surely know

Because every path that you may take

 Birthday: May 3, 1996

TOTAL BORN:	100,000	**Style #4019**
Est. Survival (2008):	10,000	

ISSUE PRICE	**$5.00**
1998 Value	**$100.00**
Year 2008 (est.)	**$750.00**

 Highly Recommended

Reduce values up to 50%
unless mint condition / mint tag.

BEANIE HUNTER TIPS: Because Chops closely resembles Fleece, he was not one of the "hot" retired Beanies in 1997. However, Chops was only made for six months and is definitely under-valued at nearly the same price he carried last year. Unless we're way off on his production figure, Chops' future price may start to take off this year.

CORAL

☼ ☼

(The Tropical Fish)

RETIRED
Dec., 1996

Coral is beautiful, as you know

These colors were chosen just for you!

Made of colors in the rainbow

Whether it's pink, yellow or blue

🎂 Birthday: March 2, 1995

TOTAL BORN:	250,000	**Style #4079**
Est. Survival (2008):	25,000	

ISSUE PRICE	$5.00
1998 Value	$75.00
Year 2008 (est.)	$400.00

 Highly Recommended

Reduce values up to 50% unless mint condition / mint tag.

BEANIE HUNTER TIPS: This tie-dyed fish is a standout in any school. In fact, he's in a class by himself. We labeled Coral a "sleeper" last year and, like Chops, his value has remained relatively stable. It won't stay that way forever, so let's go fishing for Coral right away. There is always added excitement to collecting tie-dyed toys, as unlimited color combinations are possible. If you like, you can collect a whole school of these classy deep sea Beanies, then sell off the ones that increase in value while they're still fresh.

 129

CUBBIE

(The Baseball Bear)

Cubbie used to eat crackers and honey

And what happened to him was funny

He was stung by fourteen bees

Now Cubbie eats broccoli and cheese.

ORIGINAL 9

🎂 **Birthday: November 14, 1993**

TOTAL BORN:	4,000,000	**Style #4010**
Est. Survival (2008):	400,000	

ISSUE PRICE	**$5.00**
1998 Value	**$20.00**
Year 2008 (est.)	**$125.00**

👍 Recommended

Reduce values up to 50%
unless mint condition / mint tag.

BEANIE HUNTER TIPS: Dubbed by the authors of this book as "the Baseball Bear," Cubbie was given out free to thousands of kids at Wrigley Field in 1997. First, at "Opening Day" on May 18th and then at "Back to School Day" on September 6th. (NOTE: Laminated commemorative cards were also distributed at the ball game. These are now worth $50-$100 apiece!) Cubbie is highly desirable with his first generation hang tag (at $40 - $50), though worth only a fraction of the price of Brownie.

DERBY

☼ ☼

(Fine Yarn)

1995

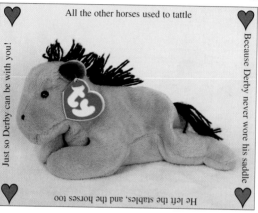

All the other horses used to tattle

Just so Derby can be with you!

Because Derby never wore his saddle

He left the stables, and the horses too

🎂 **Birthday: September 16, 1995**

TOTAL BORN:	15,000	**Style #4008**
Est. Survival (2008):	1,500	

ISSUE PRICE	**$5.00**
1998 Value	**$750.00**
Year 2008 (est.)	**$2,000.00**

 Recommended

Reduce values up to 50%
unless mint condition / mint tag.

BEANIE HUNTER TIPS: Despite his rarity, few collectors are interested in shelling out big bucks for the fine yarn Derby. (See also: Retired Mystic.) To determine if your Derby has a fine mane and tail simply count the pieces of yarn on his tail. The current Derby has approximately 20 strands, the fine yarn version only 8. Within 10 years, this elusive steed could be riding high, down the stretch. 131

1995/1997

☼ DIGGER ☼
(The Crab)

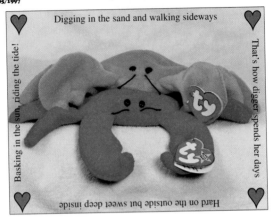

Digging in the sand and walking sideways

Basking in the sun, riding the tide!

That's how digger spends her days

Hard on the outside but sweet deep inside

Birthday: August 23, 1995

TOTAL BORN:	1,000,000*		**Style #4027**
Est. Survival (2008):	100,000		

	Orange	Red
ISSUE PRICE	$5.00	$5.00
1998 Value	$400.00	$40.00
Year 2008 (est.)	$2,000.00	$200.00

 Highly Recommended

Reduce values up to 50% unless mint condition / mint tag.

BEANIE HUNTER TIPS: *Of 1,000,000 Diggers made, no more than 40,000 of the rare orange variety exists. Of these, we'd be surprised if 1 out of 10 still has its original hang tag, some of which are first generation tags. The early Digger shares the same bright colored fabric as Goldie: The later Digger is a color match for Pinchers, Grunt, Tabasco, and Snort. We correctly guessed that the newer Digger would exercise his early retirement option in 1997. If you can dig up the dough for a perfect Orange Digger, go for it!

FLASH
(The Dolphin)

RETIRED
May, 1997

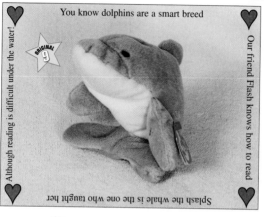

You know dolphins are a smart breed

ORIGINAL 9

Although reading is difficult under the water!

Our friend Flash knows how to read

Splash the whale is the one who taught her

Birthday: May 13, 1993

TOTAL BORN:	3,000,000	**Style #4021**
Est. Survival (2008):	300,000	

ISSUE PRICE	**$5.00**
1998 Value	**$50.00**
Year 2008 (est.)	**$250.00**

👍 Recommended

Reduce values up to 50%
unless mint condition / mint tag.

BEANIE HUNTER TIPS: News Flash: Another Fox retirement prediction comes true: The mundane Flash is replaced by the debonair Echo the Dolphin in 1997. Now, of course, Flash is the more sought after of the pair of playful aquatic mammals. Why? Because you always want what you can no longer have! As time goes by, the price of the original dolphin may swim farther and farther out to sea. 133

FLIP

(The White Cat)

Flip the cat is an acrobat

She can somersault in mid air!

She loves playing on her mat

This cat flips with such grace and flair

🎂 Birthday: February 28, 1995

TOTAL BORN: 1,000,000   **Style #4012**
Est. Survival (2008): 100,000

ISSUE PRICE	**$5.00**
1998 Value	**$50.00**
Year 2008 (est.)	**$250.00**

 Highly Recommended

Reduce values up to 50%
unless mint condition / mint tag.

BEANIE HUNTER TIPS: For some strange reason, Flip has always been harder to find than the other Kitties. Now that she's retired, she's even harder to find! (Plus, at half a hundred dollars, it is harder to find the money to buy her.) As her feline friends join the ranks of the retired, those who waited to collect the whole set will flip their lids. (Which cat will you buy next? Flip a coin. Heads it's Flip!)

☼ **FLUTTER** ☼
(The Butterfly)

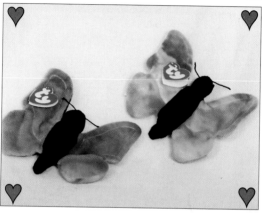

 Birthday: 1995

TOTAL BORN:	**100,000**		**Style #4043**
Est. Survival (2008):	**10,000**		

ISSUE PRICE	**$5.00**
1998 Value	**$550.00**
Year 2008 (est.)	**$2,500.00**

👍👍 **Highly Recommended**

Reduce values up to 50% unless mint condition / mint tag.

BEANIE HUNTER TIPS: Like real butterflies, the beautiful Flutter comes in colors of every shade of the rainbow. So far the authors have paid several hundred dollars for a pair of Flutters, as shown above. To our millionaire readers, we recommend collecting at least 100 examples of Flutter. Arrange these very carefully from left to right across your kitchen counter. Then call a psychiatrist.

May, 1997

☼ **GARCIA** ☼
(The Tie-Dyed Teddy)

The Beanies use to follow him around

Some even say he's legendary!

Because Garcia traveled from town to town

He's pretty popular as you can see

 Birthday: August 1, 1995

TOTAL BORN:	**500,000**	**Style #4051**
Est. Survival (2008):	**50,000**	

ISSUE PRICE	**$5.00**
1998 Value	**$50.00 – $75.00**
Year 2008 (est.)	**$300.00**

 Highly Recommended

Reduce values up to 50% unless mint condition / mint tag.

BEANIE HUNTER TIPS: Garcia is the most controversial Beanie Baby who ever lived. His birthday is a combination of rock legend Jerry Garcia's birthday (August 1, 1942) and the year Jerry died (1995.) Garcia's poem also alludes to the most well known member of the Grateful Dead. In our hit Beanie Baby song, kids chant: "But I love Garcia the best. He stands out from the rest. They put a Peace Sign on his chest." Amen, brother!

GOLDIE

(The Goldfish)

Retired
Dec., 1997

She's got the rhythm, she's got the soul

Because this goldfish likes to jam!

What more could you want in a fish bowl?

Through sound waves Goldie swam

 Birthday: November 14, 1994

TOTAL BORN: 2,000,000

Est. Survival (2008): 200,000

Style #4023

ISSUE PRICE	**$5.00**
1998 Value	**$20.00**
Year 2008 (est.)	**$150.00**

 Highly Recommended

Reduce values up to 50% unless mint condition / mint tag.

BEANIE HUNTER TIPS: We were not surprised that Goldie was retired in 1997. She was the only remaining fish of the original three (one solid, one striped, one tie-dyed) and can be found with a first generation hang tag (a good value at $75). Sooner or later, this gorgeous goldfish will turn out to be more than just a little fish in a big pond (Hint to Ty: We're awaiting the introduction of Pointy the Swordfish, Teeth the Barracuda or Dipper the Starfish!)

GRUNT
(The Razorback)

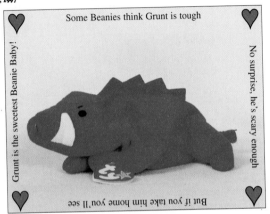

Some Beanies think Grunt is tough

Grunt is the sweetest Beanie Baby!

No surprise, he's scary enough

But if you take him home you'll see

Birthday: July 19, 1995

TOTAL BORN: 1,000,000
Est. Survival (2008): 100,000

Style #4092

ISSUE PRICE	**$5.00**
1998 Value	**$125.00**
Year 2008 (est.)	**$400.00**

 Highly Recommended

Reduce values up to 50% unless mint condition / mint tag.

BEANIE HUNTER TIPS: Due to his lack of popularity, Grunt was retired without applause last May. (We predicted 1999.) Based on his low availability even at today's high prices, it appears that we may have "grossly" over-estimated Grunt's production. This dinosaur-like creature is now on a thousand want lists, even though few kids or adults have the slightest desire to pet a razorback.

HAPPY
(The Grey Hippo)

1995

Happy the Hippo loves to wade

You know he's happy without a doubt!

In the river and in the shade

When Happy shoots water out of his snout

 Birthday: February 25, 1994

TOTAL BORN:	50,000	**Style #4061**
Est. Survival (2008):	5,000	

ISSUE PRICE	**$5.00**
1998 Value	**$450.00**
Year 2008 (est.)	**$2,500.00**

 Highly
Recommended

Reduce values up to 50%
unless mint condition / mint tag.

BEANIE HUNTER TIPS: Introduced in 1994 (shortly after the first 9 Beanies), the original Happy is rare and prized with his first generation hang tag. Although Happy is made of the same plush fabric and lightweight plastic beans as his pals, we noticed a slight sag in our livingroom floor when we left the little bugger on a coffee table overnight. (Never let Happy sit on Hoot or step on Slither.)

HOOT
(The Owl)

 ☼ ☼

Sept, 1997

Late to bed, late to rise

Like a president, do you know Whoo?

Nevertheless, Hoot's quite wise

Studies by candlelight, nothing new

 Birthday: August 9, 1995

TOTAL BORN: 3,000,000	**Style #4073**
Est. Survival (2008): 300,000	

ISSUE PRICE	**$5.00**
1998 Value	**$25.00**
Year 2008 (est.)	**$100.00**

 Recommended

Reduce values up to 50%
unless mint condition / mint tag.

BEANIE HUNTER TIPS: Although Hoot was cute, he still got the boot! (We predicted he'd be retired in 1998.) Currently not as popular as other recently retired Beanies (such as Ally and Brown New Face Teddy), Hoot is nonetheless a candidate for modest future price appreciation. As you've probably noticed, Hoot is a night owl. His eyes glow in the dark and he can hypnotize a rodent at thirty yards.

☼ HUMPHREY ☼
(The Camel)

RETIRED
Dec., 1995

🎂 **Birthday: June, 1994**

TOTAL BORN:	**25,000**	**Style #4060**
Est. Survival (2008):	**2,500**	

ISSUE PRICE	**$5.00**
1998 Value	**$1,000.00**
Year 2008 (est.)	**$5,000.00**

 Highly Recommended

Reduce values up to 50%
unless mint condition / mint tag.

BEANIE HUNTER TIPS: If you can afford to buy a mint condition Humphrey with a perfect tag (try to find a first generation tag), give yourself a pat on the hump! Most Humphreys we've seen are tagless, which generally depreciates this cushiony camel's value by 50%. However, as the knotted-tail Humphrey increases in scarcity and demand, he will become more desirable with or without a tag. Is this guy wonderful or what?

141

1996

INCH
(Felt Antennae)

Inch the worm is a friend of mine

Traveling the world without a care!

He goes so slow all the time

Inching around from here to there

Birthday: September 3, 1995

TOTAL BORN:	100,000	**Style #4044**
Est. Survival (2008):	10,000	

ISSUE PRICE	**$5.00**
1998 Value	**$100.00**
Year 2008 (est.)	**$500.00**

 Recommended

Reduce values up to 50%
unless mint condition / mint tag.

BEANIE HUNTER TIPS: Amazingly the original Inch has not increased in value since our first edition. There isn't a big difference in the appearance of Inch with thick antennae vs. Inch with thin antennae, so the scarcer version remains unappreciated. Inch's future value may crawl along for a while, but eventually it should inch up to five times its 1998 figure.

INKY
(The Tan Octopus)

Inky's head is big and round

Inky can help because he has eight!

As he swims he makes no sound

If you need a hand, don't hesitate

 Birthday: November 29, 1994

TOTAL BORN:	50,000	**Style #4028**
Est. Survival (2008):	5,000	

ISSUE PRICE	**$5.00**
1998 Value	**$450.00**
Year 2008 (est.)	**$1,500.00**

 Highly Recommended

Reduce values up to 50% unless mint condition / mint tag.

BEANIE HUNTER TIPS: As noted, the original tan Inky was either retired in 1994 (without a mouth) or in 1995 (with a mouth.) The mouthless variety is scarcer, but in general Inky is not a show-stopper. Only very serious Beanie collectors seek to acquire a tan inky to complete their collections. If you are this serious, you probably don't smile much, so try to buy Inky without a mouth. The early Inky's fabric is unique among Beanie Babies.

Dec., 1996

KIWI
(The Toucan)

Kiwi waits for April showers

I'm sure you'll guess his favorite treat!

Watching a garden bloom with flowers

There trees grow with fruit that's sweet

Birthday: September 16, 1995

TOTAL BORN:	250,000	**Style #4070**
Est. Survival (2008):	25,000	

ISSUE PRICE	**$5.00**
1998 Value	**$85.00**
Year 2008 (est.)	**$850.00**

 Highly
Recommended

Reduce values up to 50%
unless mint condition / mint tag.

BEANIE HUNTER TIPS: One of the biggest "sleepers" in the retired Beanie Kingdom! We've lowered our estimate of Kiwi's production and raised our future price prediction. Since the same-bodied Caw was much easier to manufacture in 1995-96, our investigation has revealed that Ty did not go out of its way to mass produce the more complicated Toucan. Compared to more costly Beanies (like Grunt), the modestly priced Kiwi (worth $50 last year) is definitely a deal. For that tropical feeling, why not decorate your shelves with a dozen or two Kiwis! (NOTE: Kiwi's blue bill and feet match Dark Blue Peanut's color.)

LEFTY

(The Democratic Donkey)

RETIRED
Dec., 1996

Donkeys to the left, elephants to the right

Until you realize they're spending your money!

Often seems like a crazy sight

This whole game seems very funny

🎂 **Birthday: July 4, 1996**

TOTAL BORN:	250,000	**Style #4085**
Est. Survival (2008):	25,000	

ISSUE PRICE	**$5.00**
1998 Value	**$150.00**
Year 2008 (est.)	**$1,500.00**

 Highly Recommended

Reduce values up to 50% unless mint condition / mint tag.

BEANIE HUNTER TIPS: Lefty (and Righty) have become two of the most sought-after Beanies. They are collected by kids, adults, and political memorabilia buffs, and cross all boundaries of marketability. Interestingly, Lefty comes in several varieties. His ears sometimes stand straight up, as well as pointing sideways. There's a large-headed (8" long) Lefty and a smaller size (7-1/2" long.) Plus, Lefty (and Righty) are often found without flags or with upside-down flags! (Value of such errors = $300-$500.)

LEGS
(The Frog)

  ☼   ☼

Sept., 1997

Legs lives in a hollow log

Legs will be the new friend you'll make!

ORIGINAL 9

Legs likes to play leap frog

If you like to hang out at the lake!

🎂 **Birthday: April 25, 1993**

TOTAL BORN: 5,000,000
Est. Survival (2008): 500,000

Style #4020

ISSUE PRICE	**$5.00**
1998 Value	**$25.00**
Year 2008 (est.)	**$125.00**

 Recommended

Reduce values up to 50%
unless mint condition / mint tag.

BEANIE HUNTER TIPS: As we predicted, Legs was retired in 1997. However, we've now concluded that kids have not been very kind to their pet plush frogs. So while we indicate that 500,000 examples of Legs will survive in 10 years, we also estimate that 90% of these will be missing tags and falling apart! (Hint: Buy 'em cheap while you can.) An original Legs with his first generation hang tag (rare) is a steal at $40-$50!

146

☼ LIBEARTY ☼
(The USA Bear)

Dec., 1996

I am called libearty

That's why I wear flag USA!

I wear the flag for all to see

Hope and freedom is my way

🎂 **Birthday: August, 1996**

TOTAL BORN:	500,000	**Style #4057**
Est. Survival (2008):	50,000	

ISSUE PRICE	**$5.00**
1998 Value	**$125.00**
Year 2008 (est.)	**$1,000.00**

 Highly Recommended

Reduce values up to 50%
unless mint condition / mint tag.

BEANIE HUNTER TIPS: It's worth mentioning again that Libearty was the first Beanie to debut with a poem tag. This beautiful little bear was produced to commemorate the 1996 Olympics and (like Righty and Lefty) wears the patriotic American flag. Sharing the same body as Valentino and Maple, this soft white "new face" teddy bear should be on your list of "gotta have" toys for 1998. Make sure your Libearty comes complete with a red and blue ribbon or he will not be allowed to march in official parades.

LIZZY
(The Tie-Dyed Lizard)

Dec., 1995

Her best friend Legs was at her house waiting

So Legs had to roller blade alone.

Today is the day they go roller blading

But Lizzy Lou had to stay home

 Birthday: May 11, 1995

TOTAL BORN:	20,000	**Style #4033**
Est. Survival (2008):	2,000	

ISSUE PRICE	**$5.00**
1998 Value	**$600.00**
Year 2008 (est.)	**$3,000.00**

 Highly Recommended

Reduce values up to 50% unless mint condition / mint tag.

BEANIE HUNTER TIPS: Lizzy the lizard is the rarest tie-dyed Beanie. Produced for only a few months in 1995, most Beanie maniacs know that Lizzy is rare, but they don't realize how rare she truly is! Like Flutter, Coral and Garcia, Lizzy's color combinations run the gamut from dark to light, red to blue to yellow. This version of Lizzy was only produced with a third generation heart tag. In our opinion, she is destined to wind up in the Reptilian Hall of Fame!

148

LIZZY

(The Lizard)

Dec., 1997

Lizzy loves Legs the frog

Underneath the clear blue skies!

She hides with him underlegs

Both of them search for flies

 Birthday: May 11, 1995

TOTAL BORN:	**2,000,000**	**Style #4033**
Est. Survival (2008):	**200,000**	

ISSUE PRICE	**$5.00**
1998 Value	**$20.00**
Year 2008 (est.)	**$200.00**

 Highly Recommended

Reduce values up to 50% unless mint condition / mint tag.

BEANIE HUNTER TIPS: Lizzy the Beanie Lizard is a tiny counterpart to the 280-pound Komodo dragon, the world's largest lizard. (In the Ty kingdom Lizzy was replaced by Rainbow the Chameleon and Iggy the Iguana!) Careful, kids! Unlike real lizards, if you amputate Lizzy's tail it will not grow back. Nor can it be reattached with superglue or mom's love! (NOTE: Lizzy's poem was recently improved. See tie-dyed Lizzy for the original.)

LUCKY

(The Ladybug)

Lucky the lady bug loves the lotto

Don't spend on the lotto and you'll have many!

"Someone must win" that's her motto

But save your dimes and even a penny

🎂 **Birthday: May 1, 1995**

		7-Spots	21-Spots
TOTAL BORN:	50,000*		Style #4040
Est. Survival (2008):	5,000		
ISSUE PRICE		$5.00	$5.00
1998 Value		$100.00	$450.00
Year 2008 (est.)		$750.00	$1,000.00

Lucky-7
Highly Recommended

Reduce values up to 50% unless mint condition / mint tag.

BEANIE HUNTER TIPS: Introduced in 1994 (with 7 easily lost, glued on spots), Lucky the Ladybug was not given a birthday until 1996, at which time her birthday was listed as 1995 even though she was actually born in 1994! (Weird.) Lucky is one of the most misunderstood Beanies (she's currently in therapy for multiple personality disorder) and version one is a true bargain. (See also: Current Lucky.) It is rumored that an "error Lucky-11" exists with half of Lucky's back in pure red. (*NOTE: Approximately 25,000 with 7 spots and 25,000 with 21 spots.)

MAGIC
(The Dragon)

RETIRED
Dec., 1997

Magic the dragon lives in a dream

Look up and watch her, way up high!

The most beautiful that you have ever seen

Through magic lands she likes to fly.

 Birthday: September 5, 1995

TOTAL BORN: 1,000,000   **Style #4088**
Est. Survival (2008): 100,000

ISSUE PRICE	**$5.00**
1998 Value	**$50.00**
Year 2008 (est.)	**$250.00**

 Highly Recommended

Reduce values up to 50%
unless mint condition / mint tag.

BEANIE HUNTER TIPS: The hard-to-come-by Magic is an exciting Beanie. Contrary to popular belief, this pint-sized mythical creature does not actually fly. However, he is capable of leaping up to two miles, but he only does this while kids are asleep. It is best to have this fire-breathing Beanie in an asbestos box when he's not guarding the rest of your collection. A Magic with "hot pink" thread sewn into his wings is worth $100.

MANNY

(The Manatee)

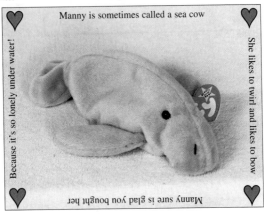

Manny is sometimes called a sea cow

Because it's so lonely under water!

She likes to twirl and likes to bow

Manny sure is glad you bought her

 Birthday: June 8, 1995

TOTAL BORN: 1,000,000   Style #4081
Est. Survival (2008): 100,000

ISSUE PRICE	**$5.00**
1998 Value	**$100.00**
Year 2008 (est.)	**$300.00**

Recommended	Reduce values up to 50% unless mint condition / mint tag.

BEANIE HUNTER TIPS: As we predicted, Manny was retired in 1997. Last May, few people shared our opinion that Manny could be worth $75 within 10 years. Shocker! He's jumped to more than that in less than a year. We still believe the charity-spirited Ty Warner should use endangered species toys to help support animal causes. At a hundred bucks a pop, Manny could make your budget an endangered species.

☼ MYSTIC ☼
(Fine Yarn)

RETIRED
1995

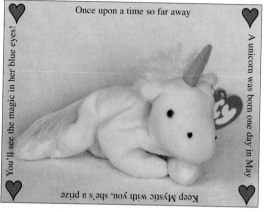

Once upon a time so far away

You'll see the magic in her blue eyes!

A unicorn was born one day in May

Keep Mystic with you, she's a prize

 Birthday: May 21, 1994

TOTAL BORN:	25,000	**Style #4007**
Est. Survival (2008):	2,500	

ISSUE PRICE	**$5.00**
1998 Value	**$200.00**
Year 2008 (est.)	**$1,200.00**

 Highly Recommended

Reduce values up to 50% unless mint condition / mint tag.

BEANIE HUNTER TIPS: Nearly as rare as the more popular (and more expensive) fine yarn Derby (also retired), the original version of Mystic can be found with a first or second generation hang tag. (NOTE: The current Mystic only comes with a third or fourth generation tag.) Because of his easily soiled white coat, Mystic may someday be even harder to find than Derby in immaculate condition. An excellent buy at $200.

NIP
(The Gold Cat)

His name is Nipper, but we call him Nip

He runs so fast he's always number one!

His best friend is a black cat named Zip

Nip likes to run in races for fun

Birthday: March 6, 1994

TOTAL BORN: 4,000,000*

Est. Survival (2008): 400,000

Style #4003

	White Face	All Gold	White Paws
ISSUE PRICE	$5.00	$5.00	$5.00
1998 Value	$350.00	$750.00	$15.00
Year 2008 (est.)	$1,500.00	$2,500.00	$100.00

 Highly Recommended

Reduce values up to 50% unless mint condition / mint tag.

BEANIE HUNTER TIPS: If you can afford to collect the rare varieties of Nip (or Zip), now is the time to step up to the scratching post. These unusual Nips are really hard to come by in perfect mint condition. Yet they have hardly appreciated in value since May, 1997. The original larger Nip has pointy pink ears, a white face and a white belly. The second type, by far the rarest, has rounded pink ears, and no white body parts. Nip #3 has white ears, whiskers and paws. (*NOTE: Of this number, only 10,000 Nips are solid gold and about 50,000 have the large white face.)

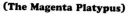

PATTI

(The Magenta Platypus)

RETIRED
1993/1995

Ran into Patti one day while walking

That would explain her extra large beak!

Believe me she wouldn't stop talking

Listened and listened to her speak

ORIGINAL 9

 Birthday: January 6, 1993

TOTAL BORN:	50,000*	**Style #4025**
Est. Survival (2008):	5,000	

ISSUE PRICE	**$5.00**
1998 Value	**$500.00**
Year 2008 (est.)	**$2,500.00**

👍 Recommended

Reduce values up to 50%
unless mint condition / mint tag.

BEANIE HUNTER TIPS: Little known to many Beanie aficionados, Patti the Platypus comes in four distinct colors. Shown above is the most common of the three rare versions of Patti, which is magenta.(NOTE: The current Patti is the purple, or fuschia, platypus.) The second rarest Patti is raspberry (Value $650). And the rarest Patti is a "deep" fuschia platypus, made only in 1993 (with only a first generation hang tag), worth $750. (*Of 50,000 made, more than half of the rare Patti's are magenta.)

☼ PEANUT ☼
(The Dark Blue Elephant)

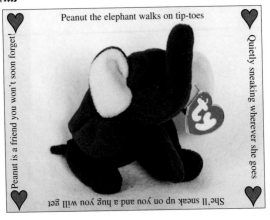

Peanut the elephant walks on tip-toes

Peanut is a friend you won't soon forget!

Quietly sneaking wherever she goes

She'll sneak up on you and a hug you will get

 Birthday: January 25, 1995

TOTAL BORN:	**2,000**	**Style #4062**
Est. Survival (2008):	**200**	(Produced only in June, 1995)

ISSUE PRICE	**$5.00**
1998 Value	**$2,500.00**
Year 2008 (est.)	**$7,500.00**

 Highly Recommended

Reduce values up to 50% unless mint condition / mint tag.

BEANIE HUNTER TIPS: Although not the rarest Beanie Baby according to original production figures (Quackers without wings, Brownie and Spot without a Spot saw the lowest original runs), the "Royal Blue" Peanut is definitely considered the "Crown Jewel" of the Beanie Baby Collection. Caution: The light blue Peanut can be dyed dark blue! Know who you are buying from! As noted above, the rare Peanut was manufactured only in June, 1995. Due to a factory error, the wrong fabric was accidentally used to make Peanut for one month.

☼ **PEKING** ☼
(The Panda)

 Birthday: 1994

TOTAL BORN: 25,000   Style #4013
Est. Survival (2008): 2,500

ISSUE PRICE	**$5.00**
1998 Value	**$1,000.00**
Year 2008 (est.)	**$4,000.00**

 Highly Recommended

Reduce values up to 50% unless mint condition / mint tag.

BEANIE HUNTER TIPS: Pandas (there are only two kinds, the giant black and white, and the red pandas) are the rarest bears in the entire world, as well as in the world of Beanies. Chilly, Peking, Cubby and Blackie are known as the four "reclining bears." Chilly is the only Ty bear with felt eye patches (a clever device) and is in great demand. (NOTE: The panda is the symbol of the World Wildlife Fund.) If you are lucky enough to own Chilly, contact your local zoning board before growing bamboo (a panda's main diet) in your back yard.

☼ QUACKER ☼
(Without Wings)

There is a duck by the name of Quackers

But he'll come to the shore to be with you!

Every night he eats animal crackers

He swims in a lake that's clear and blue

 Birthday: April 19, 1994

TOTAL BORN:	780	Style #4024
Est. Survival (2008):	78	

ISSUE PRICE	**$5.00**
1998 Value	**$1,500.00**
Year 2008 (est.)	**$6,000.00**

 Highly Recommended

Reduce values up to 50%
unless mint condition / mint tag.

BEANIE HUNTER TIPS: First tagged as "Quacker," America's favorite non-rubber ducky began his life without wings. The wingless version was off-balance and sometimes tipped over. However, it was undoubtedly re-styled for the simple reason that "Quackers without Wings" looks downright ridiculous. A type one Quacker(s) is extremely rare with its first generation tag intact.

 158

RADAR
(The Bat)

May, 1997

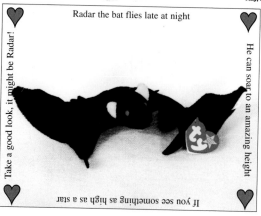

Radar the bat flies late at night

Take a good look, it might be Radar!

He can soar to an amazing height

If you see something as high as a star

🎂 **Birthday: October 30, 1995**

TOTAL BORN: 500,000   **Style #4091**
Est. Survival (2008):   50,000

ISSUE PRICE	**$5.00**
1998 Value	**$100.00**
Year 2008 (est.)	**$800.00**

 Highly Recommended

Reduce values up to 50%
unless mint condition / mint tag.

BEANIE HUNTER TIPS: With the addition of Batty the Bat last October, bat-o-maniacs can now aspire to own a complete collection of all two! (We hope Ty makes a new bat every Halloween!) The original bat, Radar, is the scarier version, with those demonlike red eyes and the sleek, sinister look of a stealth bomber. At only $100, you should definitely "zero in" on Radar!

REX

(The Tyrannosaurus)

 Birthday: 1995

TOTAL BORN:	100,000	Style #4086
Est. Survival (2008):	10,000	

ISSUE PRICE	$5.00
1998 Value	$450.00
Year 2008 (est.)	$2,000.00

 Highly Recommended

Reduce values up to 50%
unless mint condition / mint tag.

BEANIE HUNTER TIPS: While kids (and parents) anxiously await the evolution of new Ty dinosaurs, the popularity of the original three continues to soar. Unfortunately, few collectors can afford a set of dinos (or even one) at today's level, but patience prevails. (NOTE: Paleontologists still disagree as to whether the T-Rex was a predator or a scavenger.) A poem for Rex: Some call Rex the tyrant king; But in the shower he loves to sing; He prefers a burger to vegetation; He turned red in the sun on his summer vacation.

☼ RIGHTY ☼
(The Republican Elephant)

Dec., 1996

Donkeys to the left, elephants to the right

Until you realize they're spending your money!

Often seems like a crazy sight

This whole game seems very funny

 Birthday: July 4, 1996

TOTAL BORN:	250,000	**Style #4086**
Est. Survival (2008):	25,000	

ISSUE PRICE	**$5.00**
1998 Value	**$150.00**
Year 2008 (est.)	**$1,500.00**

 Highly Recommended

Reduce values up to 50% unless mint condition / mint tag.

BEANIE HUNTER TIPS: Like Lefty, Righty the elephant is one of the most sought-after Beanies. It is possible that more elephants exist than donkeys, but this is too marginal to dramatically affect future prices. We'd love to see a photo of Bill Clinton with Righty, but Bill may feel that Righty is "politically incorrect." A Righty without a flag, or an upside down flag, is worth $300-$500.

Sept., 1997

☼ SEAMORE ☼
(The Seal)

Seamore is a little white seal

She's the happiest seal in the land!

Fish and clams are her favorite meal

Playing and laughing in the sand

 Birthday: December 14, 1996

TOTAL BORN: 1,000,000
Est. Survival (2008): 100,000

Style #4029

ISSUE PRICE	**$5.00**
1998 Value	**$75.00**
Year 2008 (est.)	**$250.00**

 Highly
Recommended

Reduce values up to 50%
unless mint condition / mint tag.

BEANIE HUNTER TIPS: Now that we're seeing less of Seamore, once again collectors are running amok to pay 10 times last year's price for one of the slowest Beanies to leave toy store shelves! (A lower priced Seamore is available as a Teenie Beanie.) When a brown seal debutante glides gracefully down Ty's ice runway, we expect the handsome Seamore to become even more popular. (Keep him clean!)

✿ SLITHER ✿
(The Snake)

Dec., 1995

 Birthday: June, 1994

TOTAL BORN:	**50,000**	**Style #4031**
Est. Survival (2008):	**5,000**	

ISSUE PRICE	**$5.00**
1998 Value	**$1,000.00**
Year 2008 (est.)	**$4,000.00**

 Highly Recommended

Reduce values up to 50%
unless mint condition / mint tag.

BEANIE HUNTER TIPS: As noted above, Slither is even rarer than we thought. His top layer of skin is a darker version of the fabric on Speedy's shell and Ally's back. Caution: Don't call Slither a "yellow belly" or he may strike out with his dangerous forked tongue. Hollywood Trivia: Do you remember Slither's sleazy role in "Raiders of the Lost Ark"?

SLY
(The Brown Belly Fox)

Sly is a fox and tricky is he

He'll peek out from his den!

Please don't chase him, let him be

If you want him, just say when

 Birthday: September 12, 1996

TOTAL BORN:	**100,000**	**Style #4115**
Est. Survival (2008):	**10,000**	

ISSUE PRICE	**$5.00**
1998 Value	**$100.00**
Year 2008 (est.)	**$750.00**

 Highly Recommended

Reduce values up to 50%
unless mint condition / mint tag.

BEANIE HUNTER TIPS: To quote Peggy Gallegher, Sly the Fox has "the dubious distinction" of being the only Beanie to receive a color change almost as soon as he was released. The original Sly still carries the same $100 price tag as last May, making him one of the best buys in the retired category. However, because Sly is not as colorful as other Beanies his price may not rise significantly for a few years. (NOTE: Do not refer to the authors of this book as Sly the Foxes.)

☼ SNOWBALL ☼
(The Snowman)

Dec., 1997

There is a snowman, I've been told

Than a Beanie snowman in your hand?

That plays with Beanies out in the cold

What is better in a winter wonderland

 Birthday: December 22, 1996

TOTAL BORN:	**500,000**	**Style #4201**
Est. Survival (2008):	**50,000**	

ISSUE PRICE	**$5.00**
1998 Value	**$50.00**
Year 2008 (est.)	**$250.00**

 Highly Recommended

Reduce values up to 50%
unless mint condition / mint tag.

BEANIE HUNTER TIPS: Like all of the newer releases, the carrot-nosed Snowball the Snowman (adapted from Spooky) has been in low supply and high demand. Fearing a short lifespan, many Beanie collectors were willing to pay up to $50 for this fluffy mound of white plush (no extra charge for the plastic beans). For kids in warmer climates (Florida and California) there is an added incentive to own Snowball... You can't make your own, even on a White Christmas! Highly desirable!

RETIRED

165

☼ # SPARKY ☼
(The Dalmatian)

Sparky rides proud on the fire truck

He often gets stepped on and let's out a yelp!

Ringing the bell and pushing his luck

He gets under foot when trying to help

 Birthday: February 27, 1996

TOTAL BORN: 1,000,000	**Style #4100**
Est. Survival (2008): 100,000	

ISSUE PRICE	**$5.00**
1998 Value	**$50.00**
Year 2008 (est.)	**$200.00**

 Highly Recommended

Reduce values up to 50% unless mint condition / mint tag.

BEANIE HUNTER TIPS: It is debatable whether Sparky was retired for trademark reasons, or because Ty intends to try to create his own 101 Dalmations! Riddle: What do you get when you turn Sparky's ears and tail black? (Answer: Dotty.) Because of this close similarity, dog pack collectors can satisfy their urge for Sparky by buying up to 10 Dotty's instead.

☼ **SPEEDY** ☼
(The Turtle)

Sept., 1997

Speedy ran marathons in the past

After he bought a racing car!

Such a shame, always last

Now Speedy is a big star.

🎂 **Birthday: August 14, 1994**

TOTAL BORN: 3,000,000	**Style #4030**
Est. Survival (2008): 300,000	

ISSUE PRICE	**$5.00**
1998 Value	**$30.00**
Year 2008 (est.)	**$150.00**

 Recommended

Reduce values up to 50%
unless mint condition / mint tag.

BEANIE HUNTER TIPS: As we predicted, Speedy was retired in 1997. Slowly (perhaps very slowly), finding a mint condition turtle will become a chore. Eventually, there won't be enough Speedy's to go around. So if you missed Speedy at $5-$7, don't be afraid to "shell out" an extra twenty or so.

May, 1997

SPLASH
(The Orca Whale)

Splash loves to jump and dive

With a victory jump he'll make a splash!

He's the fastest whale alive

He always wins the 100 yard dash

 Birthday: July 8, 1993

TOTAL BORN:	4,000,000	**Style #4022**
Est. Survival (2008):	400,000	

ISSUE PRICE	**$5.00**
1998 Value	**$50.00**
Year 2008 (est.)	**$250.00**

👍 Recommended

Reduce values up to 50%
unless mint condition / mint tag.

BEANIE HUNTER TIPS: Since Splash's retirement, Sea World just hasn't been the same. Like Flash, we expect the value of this early member of the Beanie clan to continue to be in demand by America's growing number of collectors. We highly recommend Splash with a first generation hang tag at $75-$100 as one whale of a bargain!

☼ **SPOOKY** ☼
(The Ghost)

Ghosts can be a scary sight.

The best friend that Spooky can be!

But don't let Spooky bring you any fright

Because when you're alone, you will see

 Birthday: October 31, 1995

TOTAL BORN: 1,000,000	**Style #4090**
Est. Survival (2008): 100,000	

ISSUE PRICE	**$5.00**
1998 Value	**$50.00**
Year 2008 (est.)	**$200.00**

 Highly
Recommended

Reduce values up to 50%
unless mint condition / mint tag.

BEANIE HUNTER TIPS: We could be wrong, but if anything there seem to be less Spooky's around this year than last! We did not increase Ty's production figure as we question how many Spooky's were actually made. With the addition of Snowball to the Beanie line, we knew Spooky wouldn't be around very long. Truthfully, few collectors stood a ghost of a chance of acquiring more than one $5 - $7 Spooky. Keep this Beanie in the back of your closet and pay no mind to his strange, haunting noises. 169

RETIRED
1994 &
Sept, 1997

SPOT
(The Dog)

See Spot sprint, see Spot run

ORIGINAL 9

Just stand back and watch him go!

You and Spot will have lots of fun

Watch out now, because he's not slow

 Birthday: January 3, 1993

	Spot	Spot w/o Spot
TOTAL BORN: 4,000,000*		Style #4000
Est. Survival (2008): 400,000		
ISSUE PRICE	$5.00	$5.00
1998 Value	$35.00	$1,500.00
Year 2008 (est.)	$175.00	$6,000.00

 Highly
Recommended

Reduce values up to 50%
unless mint condition / mint tag.

BEANIE HUNTER TIPS: Along with Dark Blue Peanut and Quackers without wings, Spot without a spot ranks as one of the three rarest Beanie Babies. (NOTE: All three Beanies are mentioned in our song, "Spot Without A Spot," available on music CD.) Spot is one of the original nine Beanie Babies and will be a favorite forever. (*Of 4,000,000 Spots, only 1,500 were made without a Spot.)

STEG
(The Stegosaurus)

June, 1996

 Birthday: 1995

TOTAL BORN: 100,000   **Style #4087**
Est. Survival (2008): 10,000

ISSUE PRICE	**$5.00**
1998 Value	**$450.00**
Year 2008 (est.)	**$2,000.00**

 Highly
Recommended

Reduce values up to 50%
unless mint condition / mint tag.

BEANIE HUNTER TIPS: Although Bronty is the scarcest of the three dinosaurs, and Rex the most popular, Steg has the best manners. His bony plates are always spotlessly clean and he wipes his feet every time he completes his twenty-mile walk across the grassy plains and low hills. If you're rich, now is a good time to collect Steg. If you're not so rich, try to trade for him, or be patient. Ty's dinosaurs may be rejuvenated soon with new plush and beans.

Dec., 1996

STING
(The Manta Ray)

I'm a manta ray and my name is Sting

Have you ever seen something so absurd?

I'm quite unusual and this is the thing

Under the water I glide like a bird

 Birthday: August 27, 1995

TOTAL BORN:	500,000		**Style #4077**
Est. Survival (2008):	50,000		

ISSUE PRICE	**$5.00**
1998 Value	**$75.00**
Year 2008 (est.)	**$600.00**

 Highly Recommended

Reduce values up to 50% unless mint condition / mint tag.

BEANIE HUNTER TIPS: At $75, the retired Sting is currently worth only $25 more than his value last May. At this price, you may hardly feel the sting of your $100 bill being exchanged for a twenty and a five. (That is, of course, assuming you're flush with hundreds.) Seriously, we think Sting is a good Beanie to add to your collection at today's prices. Like they say, they ain't makin' 'em any more.

✿ STRIPES ✿
(The Dark Tiger)

 RETIRED
1996

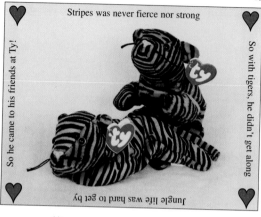

Stripes was never fierce nor strong

So he came to his friends at Ty!

So with tigers, he didn't get along

Jungle life was hard to get by

 Birthday: June 11, 1995

TOTAL BORN:	50,000	**Style #4065**
Est. Survival (2008):	5,000	

ISSUE PRICE	**$5.00**
1998 Value	**$250.00**
Year 2008 (est.)	**$1,000.00**

 Highly Recommended

Reduce values up to 50% unless mint condition / mint tag.

BEANIE HUNTER TIPS: Stripes the dark tiger is a mysteriously and highly collectable jungle beast. In addition to his darker color (gold vs. the standard caramel), the original tiger has about twice as many (more closely spaced) stripes. He also comes with a "fuzzy" belly (difficult to capture on film, see above) which is worth $600. (Very rare.)

☼ TABASCO ☼
(The Bull)

Dec. 1996

Although Tabasco is not so tall

Can you guess his favorite team?

He loves to play basketball

He is a star player in his dream

🎂 **Birthday: 1995**

TOTAL BORN:	250,000	**Style #4002**
Est. Survival (2008):	25,000	

ISSUE PRICE	**$5.00**
1998 Value	**$150.00**
Year 2008 (est.)	**$750.00**

 Highly Recommended

Reduce values up to 50% unless mint condition / mint tag.

BEANIE HUNTER TIPS: As noted last year, Tabasco was probably retired because his name is trademarked as a food product. (NOTE: Like the sauce, Ty's original bull is very hot-spirited. Don't ever pinch his nose!) Because Tabasco does not have an exact birthday (see also: Snort), he would really like to be invited to at least three or four of your other Beanies' birthday celebrations this year. It is believed that Tabasco was conceived to honor the Chicago Bulls.

TANK

(The Armadillo)

This armadillo lives in the South

Keeping his shields in good order!

Shoving a Tex-Mex in his mouth

He sure loves it south of the border

 Birthday: February 22, 1995

	Type 1	Type 2	Type 3
TOTAL BORN: 2,000,000*			**Style #4031**
Est. Survival (2008): 200,000			
ISSUE PRICE	$5.00	$5.00	$5.00
1998 Value	$125.00	$150.00	$60.00
Year 2008 (est.)	$750.00	$750.00	$250.00

 Highly Recommended

Reduce values up to 50% unless mint condition / mint tag.

BEANIE HUNTER TIPS: Now that all three versions of Tank are retired, it is time to begin expanding your armadillo army. (An average armadillo batallion contains exactly 64 grey uniformed soldiers.) To refresh your memory, Tank 1 has 7 sewn in bony plates (ribs) and was larger than the final version. The smaller Tank also has 9 plates (apparently for realism, possibly to hold together better) and less beans. Tank 3 also has 9 plates, but a firmer shell. (*9 out of 10 Tanks are Type 3.)

☼ 1997 TEDDY ☼
(Holiday)

Beanie Babies are special no doubt

Ty's holiday teddy is a magical toy!

All filled with love - inside and out

Wishes for fun times filled with joy

🎂 **Birthday: December 25, 1996**

TOTAL BORN:	250,000	**Style #4200**
Est. Survival (2008):	25,000	

ISSUE PRICE	**$5.00**
1998 Value	**$75.00**
Year 2008 (est.)	**$350.00**

 Highly Recommended

Reduce values up to 50%
unless mint condition / mint tag.

BEANIE HUNTER TIPS: Few kids awoke on Christmas morn (1997) to find this scarce Teddy under the tree. This toy is actually our old companion "Teddy New Face, Brown" (retired 10/1/97) with a new look. The red ribbon has been replaced with a white-tipped red scarf, and a white pom-pommed red Santa cap. The new Teddy is a "limited edition" which was never widely available at $5 - $7. Also, there is some speculation over the existence of Teddy's right ear. Peek-A-Boo! We've seen it in there!

TEDDY
(Brown)

Teddy wanted to go out today

After all, his best friend is you!

All of his friends went out to play

But he'd rather help whatever you do

 Birthday: 1994 (OF), Nov. 28, 1995 (NF)

TOTAL BORN:	10,000 (OF) 2,000,000 (NF)	Style #4050
Est. Survival (2008):	1,000 (OF) 200,000 (NF)	

	Old Face	New Face
ISSUE PRICE	$5.00	$5.00
1998 Value	$1,000.00	$50.00
Year 2008 (est.)	$5,000.00	$400.00

 Highly Recommended

Reduce values up to 50%
unless mint condition / mint tag.

BEANIE HUNTER TIPS: Of all 12 Teddies, six Old Face (OF) and six New Face (NF), only the relatively common New Face/Brown has a birthday. (That's because he's the only one with a fourth generation hang tag.) The original Brown Teddy is one of the three rarest in this entire group. In absolutely perfect condition he is probably the rarest. (NOTE: Only the New Face bears wear ribbons around their necks. The Brown Bear comes with a magenta ribbon.)

177

TEDDY
(Cranberry)

 Birthday: 1994 (OF), 1995 (NF)

TOTAL BORN:	20,000 (OF)	20,000 (NF)	Style #4052
Est. Survival (2008):	2,000 (OF)	2,000 (NF)	

	Old Face	New Face
ISSUE PRICE	$5.00	$5.00
1998 Value	$850.00	$750.00
Year 2008 (est.)	$4,500.00	$4,000.00

 Highly Recommended

Reduce values up to 50% unless mint condition / mint tag.

BEANIE HUNTER TIPS: Teddy Cranberry is the only "colored" bear of equal rarity in both Old Face and New Face. In fact, a cranberry-colored Teddy is the rarest color to collect. In general, New Face bears have lower production figures than Old Face bears. (See next page for style differences.) The New Face cranberry bear wears a green ribbon.

TEDDY
(Jade)

 Birthday: 1994 (OF), 1995 (NF)

TOTAL BORN:	50,000 (OF)	20,000 (NF)	Style #4057
Est. Survival (2008):	5,000 (OF)	2,000 (NF)	

	Old Face	New Face
ISSUE PRICE	$5.00	$5.00
1998 Value	$700.00	$800.00
Year 2008 (est.)	$3,500.00	$4,000.00

 Highly Recommended

Reduce values up to 50%
unless mint condition / mint tag.

BEANIE HUNTER TIPS: The dark Jade New Face Teddy is extremely hard to find in perfect condition. Many collectors are confused over the differences between Old Face (European or Squirrel Face) bears, compared to New Face (Round Face) bears. On Old Face bears, the eyes are outside the "V" seam, with smaller ears more to the sides of the bears' heads. The eyes of the New Face bears are also closer together, their heads are larger and rounder, and their bodies are fuller. New Face Teddy Jade wears a magenta ribbon.

1994/1995

 # TEDDY
(Magenta)

 Birthday: 1994 (OF), 1995 (NF)

TOTAL BORN:	50,000 (OF)	20,000 (NF)	Style #4056
Est. Survival (2008):	5,000 (OF)	2,000 (NF)	

	Old Face	**New Face**
ISSUE PRICE	$5.00	$5.00
1998 Value	$650.00	$800.00
Year 2008 (est.)	$3,500.00	$4,000.00

 Highly Recommended

Reduce values up to 50% unless mint condition / mint tag.

BEANIE HUNTER TIPS: Once again, the New Face style Magenta Teddy is the scarcer and more valuable variety. Apparently, non-brown teddies did not go over well in Europe, so Ty cut back on the number of New Face bears produced in the "odd" colors. At the same time, millions of New Face Teddies were manufactured in brown to satisfy a growing demand for Beanie Babies. (Teddy Magenta in New Face style wears a pink ribbon.)

TEDDY
(Teal)

 Birthday: 1994 (OF), 1995 (NF)

TOTAL BORN:	50,000 (OF)	10,000 (NF)	Style #4051
Est. Survival (2008):	5,000 (OF)	1,000 (NF)	

	Old Face	New Face
ISSUE PRICE	$5.00	$5.00
1998 Value	$650.00	$900.00
Year 2008 (est.)	$3,500.00	$4,500.00

 Highly Recommended

Reduce values up to 50%
unless mint condition / mint tag.

BEANIE HUNTER TIPS: Teddy the teal-colored Beanie Baby is a prize find (in any condition) in either Old Face or New Face. Why are Teddy Bears so popular? The hobby dates back to 1903, when the Steiff toy company (in Germany) began to produce mohair-covered miniature bears. A year earlier (1902), President "Teddy" Roosevelt, an avid hunter, spared the life of a bear cub, which newspapers dubbed as "teddy's bear." In a few years, Teddy Bear collecting will celebrate its 100th birthday. (NOTE: Teddy New Face Teal wears a blue ribbon.)

TEDDY
(Violet)

 Birthday: 1994 (OF), 1995 (NF)

TOTAL BORN:	50,000 (OF)	10,000 (NF)	**Style #4055**
Est. Survival (2008):	5,000 (OF)	1,000 (NF)	

	Old Face	New Face
ISSUE PRICE	$5.00	$5.00
1998 Value	$700.00	$1,000.00
Year 2008 (est.)	$4,000.00	$5,000.00

 Highly Recommended

Reduce values up to 50% unless mint condition / mint tag.

BEANIE HUNTER TIPS: Teddy Violet is considered to be the most exciting color in the Ty bear series. For Christmas 1996, Ty employees and sales reps were given a special limited edition (only 400 made) of Teddy New Face Violet. Instead of the standard green ribbon, this Teddy sometimes wears a red ribbon and does not come with a hang tag. It is identified by a different tush tag. (Bear collectors tip: If you love Ty teddies but can't scrape up the big bucks, consider "tagless teddies" at half the price.)

TRAP
(The Mouse)

June, 1995

 Birthday: 1994

TOTAL BORN:	100,000	**Style #4042**
Est. Survival (2008):	10,000	

ISSUE PRICE	**$5.00**
1998 Value	**$750.00**
Year 2008 (est.)	**$2,500.00**

 Highly Recommended

Reduce values up to 50% unless mint condition / mint tag.

BEANIE HUNTER TIPS: If you were able to capture a mint condition Trap last year at only $350, you win the cheese! Once again, this petite rodent is in very short supply and increasingly strong demand. If you are lucky enough to own this timid but enchanting mouse, protect his future value by keeping him "squeaky" clean!

TUSK
(The Walrus)

Tusk brushes his teeth everyday

And they will sparkle when you say, "Hi..."

To keep them shiny, it's the only way

Teeth are special, so you must try

🎂 **Birthday: September 18, 1995**

TOTAL BORN: 500,000
Est. Survival (2008): 50,000

Style #4076

ISSUE PRICE	**$5.00**
1998 Value	**$75.00**
Year 2008 (est.)	**$600.00**

 Highly Recommended

Reduce values up to 50% unless mint condition / mint tag.

BEANIE HUNTER TIPS: To our surprise, Tusk the Walrus is priced exactly the same as last May! With only a fraction of the mintage of other Beanies, Tusk is rated an exceptional buy. For some reason, collectors have not yet acted upon their desire to own a mint condition Tusk, and flawless specimens are relatively easy to find. Strike a deal for a pair of Tusks quickly, before his frozen value thaws.

VELVET

(The Panther)

Velvet loves to sleep in the trees

Running and jumping in the moonlight!

Lulled to dreams by the buzz of the bees

She snoozes all day and plays all night

 Birthday: December 16, 1995

TOTAL BORN: 1,000,000   **Style #4064**
Est. Survival (2008): 100,000

ISSUE PRICE	**$5.00**
1998 Value	**$15.00**
Year 2008 (est.)	**$150.00**

 Recommended

Reduce values up to 50%
unless mint condition / mint tag.

BEANIE HUNTER TIPS: One of the least expensive retired Beanie Babies, Velvet is currently experiencing a lull in popularity. Last year, she sat around in stores waiting to spring into action. However, despite Velvet's ability to jump from the cash register right into the front seat of your car, kids ignored him in favor of more colorful Stripes and Freckles, and the newer Roary. Don't expect Velvet to lie in wait at today's prices forever!

WEB
(The Spider)

🎂 **Birthday: 1994**

TOTAL BORN:	100,000	**Style #4041**
Est. Survival (2008):	10,000	

ISSUE PRICE	**$5.00**
1998 Value	**$850.00**
Year 2008 (est.)	**$3,500.00**

 Highly Recommended

Reduce values up to 50%
unless mint condition / mint tag.

BEANIE HUNTER TIPS: "Oh, what a tangled Web we weave, when first we practice to deceive." Last year we stated that Web the Spider was a "poemless" Beanie. Correction. William Shakespeare actually wrote Web's poem hundreds of years before Web (or Ty Warner) was even born! Interestingly, Web (who, by the way, is extremely rare in mint condition with mint tag) has a colored belly and a black back. In varying this theme, the newly released Spinner has a black belly and a colored back. It's easy to get caught up in Spiders!

186

ZIP
(The Black Cat)

RETIRED 1995

Keep Zip by your side all the day through

Zip will always believe in you!

Zip is good luck, you'll see it's true

When you have something you need to do

🎂 **Birthday: March 28, 1994**

TOTAL BORN:	55,000*	**Style #4004**
Est. Survival (2008):	5,500	

	White Face	All Black
ISSUE PRICE	$5.00	$5.00
1998 Value	$350.00	$1,250.00
Year 2008 (est.)	$1,500.00	$3,000.00

👍👍 Highly Recommended

Reduce values up to 50% unless mint condition / mint tag.

BEANIE HUNTER TIPS: In the same class as the rare varieties of Nip, we strongly suggest that the serious Beanie collector consider acquiring one or both of the earlier Zips in 1998. (Prices have temporarily stabilized.) The original (larger) Zip has pointy pink ears, a white face and a white belly. The second type, the rarest cat, has rounded pink ears, and no white body parts. Zip number three has white ears, whiskers and paws. (*NOTE: Of this number, only 5,000 Zips are solid black!) For comparison, the current Zip appears in photo above.

Our New Book*

THE BEANIE BABY COOKBOOK

Will Feature The Recipe "Teenie Weenies for the Teenie Beanies."

(*Coming in June – All Color – Retail $6.95)

The Beanie Baby
Collection
of
Les, Sue and Jamie Fox

The "Teenie Beanie" Babies
Introduction

From April 11th to April 25th, 1997, something very, very unusual happened at McDonald's. The average customer was less interested in hamburgers than in the free toys which accompanied them. Originally, the McDonald's Teenie Beanie promotion was scheduled to last 5 weeks, through May 15th. However, on April 19th and 20th, the nation's biggest franchise wound up running national ads on both TV and in newspapers. The ads apologized to the public for running out of miniature Beanie Babies! Beanie Mania had struck again!

According to many sources, 100 million Teenie Beanies were on hand for the McDonald's promotion. As indicated on the pages ahead, that breaks down to an even 10 million of each. Last May, we suggested that some 300 million Teenie Beanies were made. Apparently, we estimated high. However, we question the general belief that exactly 10 million of each style were issued. If this were true, why would some now be scarcer than others, with values ranging from $8 to $15? Is Pinky simply three times as popular as Lizz? Your guess is as good as ours.

All we know is that the McDonald's Teenie Beanie deal (acknowledged as the most successful McDonald's promotion ever) was everything we expected: Fun, crazy, mysterious, fattening and...profitable. (We still have a dozen frozen Happy Meals in the basement freezer.) Profitable? Indeed. As seasoned McDonald's collectors (we've got boxes and boxes of mugs and toys), we had little doubt that $2 would be less than the future value of *any* Teenie Beanie. Unfortunately, we were only able to accumulate 500 or so Beanies during the mad rush. Most are still "MIP" ("Mint In Package"), in which form their value is maximized. We also own a great McDonald's display case (see photo) as well as dozens of mint Beanie Baby Happy Meal bags.

In addition to the 10-toy display, McDonald's also raffled off thousands of 77-Beanie displays the same way we raffled off 4 free Humphreys. In mint condition, the Teenie Beanie Displays are bringing $200 to $500, the "complete set" displays $1,500 to $2,000, and a rare "media kit" box is fetching $600.

As this book goes to press, it is rumored that there will soon be a second McDonald's Teenie Beanie promotion. (McDonald's would be foolish not to do it again.) Fortunately, all of these toys are already pictured in this book (in standard size.) Needless to say, we'll be out there with the rest of the nuts accumulating more Teenie Beanies. Who knows why? We're simply "incurable collectors." Do you know what was really fun last time? Handing the McDonald's order clerk a $100 bill and saying, "Keep the change!"

(Note: McDonald's and Ty, Inc. are both located in Oak Brook, Illinois.)

Chocolate

McDonald's/Ty
**Teenie
Beanie Baby
#1**

TOTAL BORN: 10,000,000   **Birthday: April 11, 1997**
Est. Survival (2008): 250,000   **Retired: April 25, 1997**

👍👍 **Highly Recommended**	**ISSUE PRICE** $0.00 - $2.00
	1998 Value $10.00
	Year 2008 (est.) $85.00

Chops

McDonald's/Ty
**Teenie
Beanie Baby
#2**

TOTAL BORN: 10,000,000   **Birthday: April 11, 1997**
Est. Survival (2008): 250,000   **Retired: April 25, 1997**

👍👍 **Highly Recommended**	**ISSUE PRICE** $0.00 - $2.00
	1998 Value $12.00
	Year 2008 (est.) $100.00

Goldie

McDonald's/Ty
Teenie Beanie Baby
#3

| TOTAL BORN: | 10,000,000 | Birthday: April 11, 1997 |
| Est. Survival (2008): | 250,000 | Retired: April 25, 1997 |

Highly Recommended

ISSUE PRICE	$0.00 - $2.00
1998 Value	$8.00
Year 2008 (est.)	$60.00

Lizz

McDonald's/Ty
Teenie Beanie Baby
#4

| TOTAL BORN: | 10,000,000 | Birthday: April 11, 1997 |
| Est. Survival (2008): | 250,000 | Retired: April 25, 1997 |

Highly Recommended

ISSUE PRICE	$0.00 - $2.00
1998 Value	$8.00
Year 2008 (est.)	$75.00

Patti

McDonald's/Ty
**Teenie
Beanie Baby**
#**5**

TOTAL BORN: 10,000,000   Birthday: April 11, 1997
Est. Survival (2008): 250,000   Retired: April 25, 1997

Highly Recommended	**ISSUE PRICE**	**$0.00 - $2.00**
	1998 Value	**$10.00**
	Year 2008 (est.)	**$85.00**

Pinky

McDonald's/Ty
**Teenie
Beanie Baby**
#**6**

TOTAL BORN: 10,000,000   Birthday: April 11, 1997
Est. Survival (2008): 250,000   Retired: April 25, 1997

Highly Recommended	**ISSUE PRICE**	**$0.00 - $2.00**
	1998 Value	**$15.00**
	Year 2008 (est.)	**$100.00**

Quacks

McDonald's/Ty
Teenie Beanie Baby
#**7**

TOTAL BORN: 10,000,000
Est. Survival (2008): 250,000
Birthday: April 11, 1997
Retired: April 25, 1997

Highly Recommended

ISSUE PRICE	$0.00 - $2.00
1998 Value	$8.00
Year 2008 (est.)	$60.00

Seamore

McDonald's/Ty
Teenie Beanie Baby
#**8**

TOTAL BORN: 10,000,000
Est. Survival (2008): 250,000
Birthday: April 11, 1997
Retired: April 25, 1997

Highly Recommended

ISSUE PRICE	$0.00 - $2.00
1998 Value	$8.00
Year 2008 (est.)	$60.00

Snort

McDonald's/Ty
Teenie
Beanie Baby
#9

TOTAL BORN: 10,000,000   **Birthday:** April 11, 1997
Est. Survival (2008): 250,000   **Retired:** April 25, 1997

Highly Recommended

ISSUE PRICE		$0.00 - $2.00
1998 Value		$8.00
Year 2008 (est.)		$60.00

Speedy

McDonald's/Ty
Teenie
Beanie Baby
#10

TOTAL BORN: 10,000,000   **Birthday:** April 11, 1997
Est. Survival (2008): 250,000   **Retired:** April 25, 1997

Highly Recommended

ISSUE PRICE		$0.00 - $2.00
1998 Value		$8.00
Year 2008 (est.)		$60.00

A CLASS ACT! Fifth grade students at Sandpiper Shores Elementary in Boca Raton, Florida (with teacher, Chris Benavides) display their favorite Beanie Babies, plus their favorite Beanie Baby Handbook. (See "Acknowledgments" page for drawing by Beanie artist Danielle Tucceri.)

BEANIE BABIES BREAK LANGUAGE BARRIER. According to language specialist, Cappi Duncan, these Hispanic students from Beaumont California learned English at twice the normal speed in order to read Beanie poems and The Beanie Baby Handbook! The group is known as "Kyle's Kids" thanks to CBS-TV news anchor Beanie lover Kyle Kraska. (left to right: Maria Valenzuela, Adelita Olvera, Jonathan Sanchez, Melissa Garcia, Kyle Kraska, Orlando Salmeron and Maricella DeLaTorre.)

More 4 Kids!

Turn page for more games, puzzles & Beanie Baby Checklist. (Also lyrics to "Beanie Baby Songs")

Kid Beanie™

(Top left) Meghan, Jessica and Tyler Just, with Michael and Christina Rothenburg, decorate Christmas tree with familiar ornaments. (Submitted by "Beanie Nana" Christine Thompson of West Palm Beach, Florida.

(Top right) Brett and Brieann Harms examine new inventory for Beanie Mom's floral gift shop in Richfield, Minnesota.

(Bottom) Jessica and Kara Costanzo, with Lauren Fink, visit Forever Green shop in Mall of America while performing Beanie songs in native garb.

Connect The "Beanies" And Draw Beanie The Pirate's Favorite Baby

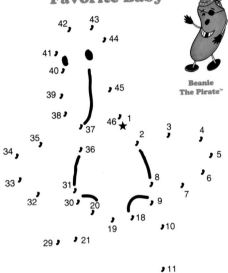

Beanie The Pirate™

Find The Hidden Beanies In The Beanie Tree Picture

Drawing by Gerald Bauman

Wait! That's the easy part. Now place the 12 names in the slots below (in alphabetical order) to unscramble the circled letters and answer this tricky question:

Which prize did Chocolate win at the country fair?

Hint: Alphabetize the words on a separate sheet of paper first.
WARNING: Better us a pencil, not a pen!

1. ☐◯◯☐☐☐
2. ☐☐☐☐☐☐
3. ☐☐☐☐☐◯
4. ☐☐☐☐☐
5. ☐◯☐☐☐
6. ◯☐☐☐
7. ☐◯☐◯
8. ◯◯☐☐☐☐☐
9. ◯☐☐☐☐☐
10. ◯☐☐◯☐
11. ☐◯☐☐☐
12. ☐☐◯☐☐

Rearrange Letters Below

Ⓢ ◯ Ⓔ ◯ ◯ Ⓞ   Ⓠ ◯ ◯ Ⓘ ◯   Ⓜ ◯ ◯ ◯ Ⓔ

Answers see page 214

 199

Professor
Beanie™

Help Professor Beanie Find The Two Matching Hippitys

Beanie Baby Crossword

(Answers on page 214.)

Across

1. ___ of birth
5. All Beanies have them
9. Hoot the ___
12. Used to catch Goldie
13. A small child
14. Chief Executive Officer (abbr.)
15. The 3rd and 2nd letters in the bee's name
17. Teenie Beanie Baby (abbr.)
18. Playing cards higher than Kings
20. Opposite of "on"
22. ___ and Eve
23. Short for information
24. *Peter* ___
27. ___ the Worm
29. ___ and downs
30. Police enforce this
33. The last word in Baldy's poem
34. A malicious look
37. A lyric poem
38. ___ the Dog
39. You sleep in this
40. How many Teenie Beanies are there?
43. A type of beer
44. ___ eanie
45. What a cowboy might say
47. Chip ___ Cat
50. An indefinitely long period of time
51. Rhymes with "hoop"
54. The color of Pinchers
55. The brown bunny's name
56. Oklahoma (abbr.)
57. ___ aby

Down

2. Tank is an ___
3. Kiwi the ___
4. *Mister* ___
6. Past tense of "eat"
7. Opposite of stop
8. Rhymes with "puff"
9. Inky the ___
10. The retired spider
11. Toss a ball slowly
16. The 4th and 5th letters of retired bull's name
19. Einstein's theory of relativity (___ = ___ ___ ²)
20. The opposite of 20 Across
21. Sly the ___ (also the authors of this book)
25. Everyone goes "___" for Beanie Babies
26. Three letters on a compass
28. You take Derby ___ riding
30. Pinchers the ___
31. Lemon ___ ___ ___ (one word)
32. To marry
35. To make able
36. Fish resembling a snake
38. What Spooky would say
40. Beanie Babies creator
41. Baldy the ___
42. New Hampshire (abbr.)
43. Stinky's defense
48. Garden tool
49. The ___
52. Derby eats ___ ___ ts
53. Postscript (abbr.)

KIDS' LETTERS

Here are quotes from some of the most entertaining letters we received from Beanie fans across America.

"Spinz"
Jill Rajevich
Wilmington, DE

"Blinky"
Donna Wermann
Laurys Station, PA

"I would love to see a loon named Lenny because the loon is the Minnesota state bird and my dad's name is Lenny."

Stephen Hingos, Golden Valley, MN

"I'm obsessed with Beanie Babies, but I can't find them anywhere."

Robert Bonadies, Rocky Hill, CT

Tito Porras

Tito Porras second grade

"I think that all the people at Ty should be nicely rewarded with a Great BIG Hug for making children all across the globe happy."

Katie Chase, Grand Rapids, MI

"We love the idea of a Golden Retriever (we have one) as a beanie, however, we don't think the name 'Blondie' is appropriate. We think 'Sandy,' 'Buddy,' or 'Max' would be much more appealing."

Annie and Darby Putnma, Horseheads, NY

"I heard if you make up a new beanie baby name, you get all the beanie babies."

Jared Thomas, Manalapan, NJ

Kristina Debold, Olney, MD

A Tribute to "Smokie"

Dear TY Inc.,

I love all the beanie babies the same. I am a big fan and collector. Maby my favorite beanie is the Fox, Sly. I think sly needs black feet and a white tipod his tail. I know a lot about foxes. I also have a sugestion for a new beinie. A gray hamster named Smokie. I used to have a gray hamster named Smokie but he chewed through the cage and we think while he was our the art insulation in a room we are building and Smokie died very sad but it It made me would make me extremly make Smokie a happy if you beanie.

Your friend,

Kelly Hourigan
Kelly Hourigan

P.S. Please write back and tell me what shider you thought.

Kelly Hourigan, Lake Zurich, IL

Robbie Cohen
Hewlett Harbor, NY

"I have a idea for a new Beanie Baby, Pecks. I got the idea when a baby pigeon with a broken wing came to my house. I called the animal shelter. It got a good vote."

Shane Kalminski, East Pointe, MI

Stevie Belchak
Shelton, CT

"I've been trying to find the extremly old and retired beanies, namely Slither & Trap, but alas (I'm being dramatic), I found none."

Sara Rosengarten, Cedarhurst, NY

Kathy Miu,
Syosset, NY

"My idea for a Beanie Baby is an alien. It is bright green. It has 3 eyes, with a little antenna coming out from the top of his head. It has a shirt and the shirt says 'PLANET ZO-BROB.' It's name is Marvin."

Nicholas A. Fountain, Creamery, PA

Ty Beanie Babies everywhere,
All the children can do is buy and stare,
Beanie Babies are carefully laid in shopping carts,
while they are placed in the children's hearts!

Future Beanie Babies...

...through the eyes of children

Bugs the Ant Eater

Danny Root, West Bloomfield, MI

Wiley the Rotwiler

Lindsay Harrington, Sylvania, OH

Mickey the Beagle

Lindsay Hassert, Wayne, NJ

Fins the

Melanie Badmann, Farmington Hills, MI

Duckie TieDied

Carly & Zachary Hill, Nashville, TN

Pip the Gray Cat

Jill Rajevich, Wilmington, DE

Snowflake the Cat

Lindsey E.

Oreo the Border Collie

Mindy Gray, Baldwin, NY

Needles the Porcupine

Laura Stenulis, Schnecksville, PA

Lily the Tuxhed Cat

Ashley Rathfon, Longview, TX

Elimay Sue the Cow

Stephanie Millward, Omaha, NE

Teenie and Tiny the Elephants

Jillian Rajevich

Petunia the

Roxanne Arnold, Sunny Vale, CA

Yagi the Goat

Donny Dietz, Scarsdale, NY

Snowy the Snow Leopard

Clayton Jameson, Olathe, KS

Shelly the Snail

Christopher Buklerewicz, Leominster, MA

Wings the Dragonfly

Maura Boghosian, Burlington, MA

Iggy the Iguana

Kelsey Ward

Marty the Martian

Jennifer Brammer, Melrose, MA

Jumpy The Grasshopper

Kristen Mennie, Howell, NJ

Scooter the Snail

Shannon Latham, Cortland, OH

Future Beanie Babies We'd Like To See

Thanks to all the thousands of kids who wrote to us last year with votes for their favorite Future Beanies. (Sorry, we cannot answer letters personally.)

Here are the 10 "winners," whose names we are forwarding to Ty, Inc. for consideration as real future Beanies:

"Top 10" Future Beanie Requests	Votes
1. Blondie the Golden Retriever*	1,474
2. Colors the Peacock	1,126
3. Midnight the Black Lab	1,005
4. Sprint the Cheetah	961
5. Ice the Arctic Fox	940
6. Cuddles the Llama	889
7. Fluffy the Poodle	861
8. Harley the Roadrunner	829
9. Pal the Beagle	798
10. Bugs the Anteater	716
TOTAL:	**9,599**

*Note: Blondie the Golden Retriever is so popular that *Collecting Figures Magazine* mistakenly listed Blondie as a real Beanie Baby in its December 1997 issue at $60!

We've also come up with 36 new ideas for Future Beanie Babies. This is not a contest. Just keep this list handy to so see how well our predictions do.

Beefy the Buffalo
Biscuit the Dog
Blush the Cardinal
Bumpy the Toad
Choke the Boa
Creepy the Caterpillar
Dart the Chipmunk
Dizzy the Possum
Early the Robin
Elvis the Blue Suede Teddy
Fuzzy the Grizzly
Goliath the Dragonfly

Henrietta the Hen
Itchy the Flea
Muscles the Boxer
Oscar the Ox
Pain the Wasp
Pitchfork the Tazmanian Devil
Ralph the Rottweiler
Road the Hog
Rusty the Orangutan
Slink the Lynx
Slow the Snail
Speckles the Guinea Pig

Spirit the Angel
Spring the Grasshopper
Squawk the Parrot
Squeeze the Beetle
Stretch the Ferret
Sugar the Ant
Swat the Fly
Swoop the Hawk
Trapeze the Chimp
Trek the Starfish
Vanilla the Moose
Vicious the Vulture

Beanie Baby Word Search

Look forward, backward, up, and down
for your favorite Beanie names.

```
S  Q  U  E  A  L  E  R  Y  L  L  O  J  V
E  U  B  A  L  J  C  S  B  U  M  B  L  E
A  A  E  R  L  T  H  T  Y  Y  Z  Z  I  L
M  C  W  S  Y  B  O  D  G  R  U  N  T  V
O  K  E  C  A  E  P  K  G  O  L  D  I  E
R  E  X  Y  T  I  P  P  I  H  K  N  A  T
E  R  B  H  C  N  I  D  Z  Y  F  F  U  T
O  S  E  P  I  R  T  S  I  D  S  L  H  L
C  U  R  L  Y  E  Y  G  P  D  E  I  S  E
S  T  E  G  O  B  S  I  A  E  L  P  A  M
A  C  L  E  G  S  L  W  T  T  B  I  L  K
B  A  L  D  Y  P  Y  T  T  A  B  W  P  S
A  W  R  E  V  O  R  P  I  N  U  I  S  U
T  R  O  N  S  T  R  A  P  Z  B  K  G  T
```

(Answers on page 214)

ALLY	INCH	SPOT
BALDY	JOLLY	SQUEALER
BATTY	KIWI	STEG
BERNIE	LEGS	STRIPES
BUBBLES	LIZZY	TABASCO
BUMBLE	MAPLE	TANK
CAW	MEL	TEDDY
CURLY	NIP	TRAP
DOBY	PATTI	TUFFY
EARS	PEACE	TUSK
ECHO	REX	TWIGS
FLIP	ROVER	QUACKERS
GOLDIE	SEAMORE	VELVET
GRUNT	SLY	WEB
HIPPITY	SNORT	ZIGGY
HOPPITY	SPLASH	ZIP

Beanie Baby Birthdays

Were You Born on the Same Day as a Beanie?

New Birthdays For 1998 Toys in Red

JANUARY

Jan. 3, 1993	Spot
Jan. 6, 1993	Patti
Jan. 13, 1996	Crunch
Jan. 14, 1997	Spunky
Jan. 15, 1996	Mel
Jan. 18, 1994	Bones
Jan. 21, 1996	Nuts
Jan. 25, 1995	Peanut
Jan. 26, 1996	Chip

FEBRUARY

Feb. 1, 1996	Peace
Feb. 13, 1995	Stinky
Feb. 13, 1995	Pinky
Feb. 14, 1994	Valentino
Feb. 17, 1996	Baldy
Feb. 20, 1996	Roary
Feb. 22, 1995	Tank
Feb. 25, 1994	Happy
Feb. 27, 1996	Sparky
Feb. 28, 1995	Flip

MARCH

Mar. 2, 1995	Coral
Mar. 6, 1994	Nip
Mar. 8, 1996	Doodle
Mar. 8, 1996	Strut
Mar. 14, 1994	Ally
Mar. 19, 1996	Seaweed
Mar. 21, 1996	Fleece
Mar. 28, 1994	Zip

APRIL

Apr. 3, 1996	Hoppity
Apr. 4, 1997	Hissy
Apr. 12, 1996	Curly
Apr. 18, 1995	Ears
Apr. 19, 1994	Quackers
Apr. 23, 1993	Squealer
Apr. 25, 1993	Legs
Apr. 27, 1993	Chocolate

MAY

May 1, 1995	Lucky
May 1, 1996	Wrinkles
May 2, 1996	Pugsly
May 3, 1996	Chops
May 10, 1994	Daisy
May 11, 1995	Lizzy
May 13, 1993	Flash
May 15, 1995	Snort
May 19, 1995	Twigs
May 21, 1994	Mystic
May 28, 1996	Floppity
May 30, 1996	Rover

JUNE

June 1, 1996	Hippity
June 3, 1996	Freckles
June 8, 1995	Bucky
June 8, 1995	Manny
June 11, 1995	Stripes
June 15, 1996	Scottie
June 17, 1996	Gracie
June 19, 1993	Pinchers
June 27, 1995	Bessie

JULY

July 1, 1996	Scoop
July 1, 1996	Maple
July 2, 1995	Bubbles
July 4, 1996	Lefty
July 4, 1996	Righty
July 8, 1993	Splash
July 14, 1996	Ringo
July 15, 1994	Blackie
July 19, 1995	Grunt
July 20, 1995	Weenie

AUGUST

Aug. 1, 1995	Garcia
Aug. 9, 1995	Hoot
Aug. 9, 1997	Iggy
Aug. 13, 1996	Spike
Aug. 14, 1994	Speedy
Aug. 17, 1995	Bongo
Aug. 23, 1995	Digger
Aug. 27, 1995	Sting
Aug. 28, 1997	Pounce

SEPTEMBER

Sept. 3, 1995	Inch
Sept. 3, 1996	Claude
Sept. 5, 1995	Magic
Sept. 9, 1997	Bruno
Sept. 12, 1996	Sly
Sept. 16, 1995	Kiwi
Sept. 16, 1995	Derby
Sept. 18, 1995	Tusk
Sept. 21, 1997	Stretch

OCTOBER

Oct. 1, 1997	Smoochy
Oct. 3, 1996	Bernie
Oct. 9, 1996	Doby
Oct. 12, 1996	Tuffy
Oct. 14, 1997	Rainbow
Oct. 16, 1995	Bumble
Oct. 17, 1996	Dotty
Oct. 22, 1996	Snip
Oct. 28, 1996	Spinner
Oct. 30, 1995	Radar
Oct. 31, 1995	Spooky

NOVEMBER

Nov. 3, 1997	Puffer
Nov. 6, 1996	Pouch
Nov. 9, 1996	Congo
Nov. 14, 1993	Cubbie
Nov. 14, 1994	Goldie
Nov. 20, 1997	Prance
Nov. 21, 1996	Nanook
Nov. 27, 1996	Gobbles
Nov. 28, 1995	Teddy Brown
Nov. 29, 1994	Inky

DECEMBER

Dec. 2, 1996	Jolly
Dec. 8, 1996	Waves
Dec. 12, 1996	Blizzard
Dec. 14, 1996	Seamore
Dec. 16, 1995	Velvet
Dec. 19, 1995	Waddle
Dec. 21, 1996	Echo
Dec. 22, 1996	Snowball
Dec. 24, 1995	Ziggy
Dec. 25, 1996	'97 Teddy

Lyrics to "BEANIE BABY SONGS"

All songs copyright 1997 by Les and Sue Fox

BEANIE BABIES ARE HERE TO STAY!

(The "Unofficial" Beanie Baby Song)

I want it! I want it! I want a Beanie Baby!
Mommy! Please get it! Get me a Beanie Baby!
Want it! I want it! I want a Beanie Baby
now...now...Now! Now! Now!

I used to play with Barbie Dolls. I used to collect
Cabbage Patch Kids. I used to like those
ugly Trolls.
But I threw them all away.
There's a brand new toy for today!

BEANIES! They've got a place in my heart.
BEANIES! You'll never tear us apart.
Show me the Beanie Babies! I love the
Beanie Babies!
Show me the Beanie Babies! And don't ever
take them away,
Cause...
Beanie Babies...Beanie Babies...
Beanie Babies are here to stay!

I love my cats, Nip, Zip and Flip.
I love my rabbits, especially Ears.
I love my dogs, Wrinkles and Bones.
But I love Garcia the best.
He stands out from all the rest.
They put a Peace Sign on his chest.

(Repeat chorus)

I love my poems and my heart shaped tags.
I cut 'em off and I save 'em in bags.
Beanies are the birthday toys.
They're loved by girls and by boys.
My little animals don't make much noise.
Oh...

(Repeat chorus)

BEANIE BABIES EVERYWHERE!

In my refrigerator, behind the milk and
cheese,
There lives an alligator who says "Thank
you" and "Please"!
And underneath my underwear, below my
yellow socks,
A cute raccoon named Ringo hangs out with
Sly the Fox.

Oh, Beanie Babies everywhere! Beanie
Babies more!
Beanie Babies everywhere, they're knocking
at my door!

I open up my lunch box, and what do you
think I find?
A squirrel and a pelican, driving me out of
my mind!
I go into the bathroom, just to wash my face
And a beaver and an octopus are messing up
the place!

(Repeat chorus)

I cannot get away from them, they're
everywhere I go.
A camel ate my father's coat, a lobster bit
my toe!
But luckily I have a plan to end this
Beanie war.
My mother bought a great big broom
to sweep them out the door!

Oh, Beanie Babies everywhere! Beanie
Babies more!
Beanie Babies everywhere, especially
on the floor!
Oh, Beanie Babies everywhere! Beanie
Babies more!
Beanie Babies everywhere, they're knocking
at my door!
Beanie Babies everywhere,
they're knock...ing...at...my...door!
Let me out of here!

**See "A Bear For The Princess" lyrics on page 12.
Another great song from Les and Sue Fox.
Ask for it at your favorite store!**

Lyrics to "BEANIE BABY SONGS"

All songs copyright 1997 by Les and Sue Fox

CUBBIE'S FIRST HOME RUN

It was a beautiful day at Wrigley Field.
The seats were packed, the game
was real.
And Cubbie stepped right up to the plate
And took a practice swing.

It was a beautiful drive past second base.
The crowd went wild when they saw
his face.
And a polar bear in the box seats yelled,
"Man! That's the way to go!"

And the whole darn team raised up
their arms,
And did a Cubbie wave,
As the little bear scooted down the first
base line.
And Cubbie's Mom and Dad stood up
and said,
"Is our boy brave?
He's playing baseball for the very first
time!"

It was a beautiful slide at second base,
But the effort was a total waste.
Cause the throw was wide, so Cubbie
raced
Down to the third base coach.
The coach told Cubbie to smile and
keep alert.
When the ball arrived, it hit the dirt.
As Cubbie rounded third and
headed home,
The crowd was on its feet!

When Cubbie reached the dugout,
puffing hard,
They slapped his back.
And a pretty little bear cub kissed him on
his cheek.
The Chicago press took color pictures
for the Sunday news.
It was the first home run
In nearly thirteen weeks!

It was a beautiful day at Wrigley Field.
The seats were packed, the game
was real.
And Cubbie refused a tobacco pouch
For a great big honey jar!

MEET THE BEANIES!
(The Alphabet Marching Song)

"A" is for Ally, my Alligator pal!
"B" is for Bessie, she lives in a corral!
"C" is for Caw, who crows when he eats corn!
"D" is for Derby, who gallops every morn!

(Hup, two, three four! Hup, two, three four...)

"E" is for my elephant, Peanut his name
"F" is for Freckles, who wants to play a game
With Gracie or Goldie, or maybe even Grunt.
"H" is for Hippity, who's always on an Easter
Egg hunt!

It's time to meet the Beanies,
It's time to have a ball!
It's time to meet the Beanies...
From to A to Z, you definitely
Will love them...one and all!

"I" is for Inky, shake tentacles with him!
"J" is for Jolly, give his mustache a trim!
"K" is for Kiwi, his colors are so bright!
"L" is for Lefty, his flag is on the right!
"M" is for Mystic, watch out for his
sharp horn!
"N" is for Nanook, it snowed when he
was born!
"O" is for the other toys missing from
this song!
"P" is for Pinky, gosh, those legs are long!

(Repeat chorus)

"Q" is for Quackers, I love his orange bill!
"R" is for Ringo, his face mask is a thrill!
"S" is for Spooky, he really is unique!
"T" is for Tabasco, who snorts but
doesn't speak!
"U" and "X" and "Y" are missing from the
group!
But Valentino's kisses will throw you
for a loop!
"W" is for Waddle, my penguin is a trip!
And "Z" is for Ziggy, or possibly for Zip!

And now you've met the Beanies,
The big ones and the small!
Yes, you've met all the Beanies!
So you tell me, from A to Z,
Isn't it true, you definitely,
Love those Beanies, one and all?

Lyrics to "BEANIE BABY SONGS"

All songs copyright 1997 by Les and Sue Fox

BONGO AND CONGO

Deep in the jungle (Bom-bom-bah-bom-bom)
A gorilla named Congo
    (Bom-bom-bah-bom-bom)
Had a best friend, *(Drum sounds continue)*
A monkey named Bongo.
But poor Bongo
Was accident prone.
How do you like that?

In the shade of a palm tree
    (Bom-bom-bah-bom-bom)
They shared a banana
    (Drum sounds continue)
Till Bongo reached up
And a coconut fell.
Hit Congo in the head
Just like a hammer.
How do you like that?

And Bongo said:
"It was an accident.
I didn't mean to dent
Your great big, hairy skull."
And Congo said:
"You better beat it, man!
Run as fast as you can.
And don't come back...for the rest of your
    natural life."

So Bongo ran away
    (Bom-bom-bah-bom-bom)
And gathered his friends:
Roary the Lion,
Stripes the Tiger,
Spike the Rhino,
Happy the Hippo.
How do you like that?

And they all came back
    (Bom-bom-bah-bom-bom)
To the coconut tree,
And Bongo told Congo,
"My friends will protect me!"
And Congo told Bongo:
"I'm feeling much better.
I guess I was
Under the weather,
There's no reason to fight."
So the animals played checkers, right in
    the jungle,
All through the night! How do you like that?

LOST AND FOUND

Well, I went down to the lost and found
And I wiped the tears from my eyes.
They gave me a form, and a pen and a
    chair,
And said: "Fill this out three times."
When I handed back the papers
The lady behind the desk
Took a look at me all by myself
And said, "Honey, you need a rest."
So I stood up straight, and told her, "This
    can't wait.

"I've just lost my best friend."
When she looked at the name,
She said, "No one's to blame.
All good things must come to an end."
And she handed me five dollars,
And she gave me a great big smile.
Then she reached for my hand,
But she didn't understand
That a Beanie Baby's just like a child.

I handed back the five-dollar bill
Fearing things would only worsen.
It's been three days since Patti the
    Platypus
Has been a missing person.
Oh, I tried and I tried to tell her
How much Patti means to me.
I could never replace that cute purple face.
And I don't even want to try.

So I started to the leave the lost and found
And I felt my heart in my hand.
When a handsome young boy
Brushed against my dress
With something very soft in his hand.
I couldn't believe my very own eyes
When he set Patti down on the desk.
And it wasn't my fault that I needed
    smelling salt.
I'd been put through the greatest test.

Lyrics to "BEANIE BABY SONGS"

All songs copyright 1997 by Les and Sue Fox

BLACKIE THE ICE CREAM BEAR

Welcome to the circus! Listen to the gun!
The dancing bear is dancing, but he's not
    having fun.
A ring around his ankle, a muzzle on
    his nose,
You never see him smiling anywhere
    he goes.

But on Sunday he eats ice cream,
A big vanilla cup.
Chocolate sprinkles and whipped cream,
And a cherry on the top.

Blackie is a circus bear. The circus is his life
He hasn't any children, he doesn't have a
    wife.
His father was a dancing bear, a prisoner
    of man.
He never knew his mother, or his
    brother Dan.

But on Sunday he eats ice cream,
And dreams of being free.
Selling sundaes in an ice cream store
And making history.

Ten years have passed for Blackie. He's still
    a circus bear.
He's gained ten pounds, he dances slow.
    There's grey in his black hair.
The people cheer, but not as loud. They've
    seen it all before.
And then one day a rich young man comes
    through the Big Top door.

The young man's name is Johnny.
He wants to buy the bear.
He says he owns an ice cream store
And needs a helping hand.

The circus bear learns new tricks. He even
    makes a float.
He eats up all the profits, and drips some on
    his toes.
The ring and muzzle on the wall, Johnny
    and Blackie have a ball.
And now you see him smiling everywhere
    he goes.

DON'T ASK HIM WHY
(His Name Is Ty)

Why does Derby the horse
Come with coarse and fine hair?
Why are there "old face"
And "new face" teddy bears?
The kids all want to know
But their parents just don't care.
There has to be an answer,
But no one knows where.

Don't ask him why.
His name is Ty.
And he'd never tell a lie.
Don't ask him why.
His name is Ty.
Cause he'll just tell you the answers
Are up in the sky!

Why did Digger the crab
turn from orange to red?
What happened to the horn
On top of Mystic's head?
And why did Stripes the tiger
Go to light from dark?
Was it all done on purpose
Or was it just a lark?
Don't ask him why. His name is Ty.

(Repeat chorus)

Why did they put more spots
on Lucky's back?
And why is Quackers' name
Also Quacker and Quacks?
Tell me, why do lots of Beanie cats
rhyme with Nip and Zip?
But the dogs don't rhyme at all!
Don't ask him why. His name is Ty.

(Repeat chorus)

Lyrics to "BEANIE BABY SONGS"

All songs copyright 1997 by Les and Sue Fox

THE BEANIE BABY DINOSAUR STOMP
(Chomp! Chomp! Chomp! Chomp!)

Do the Rex! (Da-da-da-da-da-da-da!)
Wrap your hands around your necks!

Do the Bronty! (Da-da-da-da-da-da-da!)
You look like Harry Belafonte!

Do the Steg! (Da-da-da-da-da-da-da!)
Jump up and down and shake your leg!

Now chomp your teeth!
And act real crazy!
Cause you are doin'
The Beanie Baby...Dinosaur Stomp!
(Chomp! Chomp! Chomp! Chomp!)

Do the Rex!
Open your jaws and stretch your necks!

Do the Bronty!
Spin 'round like Harry Belafonte!

Do the Steg!
Slap your hands across your legs!

Now chomp your teeth!
And act real crazy!
And keep on doin'
The crazy Beanie Baby...Dinosaur Stomp!
(Chomp! Chomp! Chomp! Chomp!)

(Dance steps self-explanatory!
Move arms like Rex, then like Bronty,
Wiggle side to side like Steg, stomp feet,
and act like Harry Belafonte!)

SPOT WITHOUT A SPOT
(The Beanie Baby Blues)

I have a spot
For a "Spot Without A Spot."
Although I have a lot, I have not...
Got a Spot Without A Spot.

I need a Peanut in Royal Blue.
What can I do
To get you... to get me
That royal blue?

Life will go on
Without my Beanie friends.
But when they're gone
Can you ever make amends...

For not getting me
A Quackers Without Wings.

My young heart sings
For a bright yellow Quackers Without Wings!

(Repeat chorus)

For not getting me
A Quackers Without Wings.
My young heart sings
For a bright yellow Quackers Without Wings!
(And a black and white Spot Without A Spot.)
(And a beautiful Peanut Royal Blue.)
Oh, tell me, what can I do?
If you buy those toys I always will love you.
If you buy those toys...I always...will...love...you!

I NEVER MET A BEANIE BABY I DIDN'T LIKE

I never met a Beanie Baby I didn't like.
All my other toys can go take a hike.
I never met a Beanie Baby I didn't like.
That's why I need a hundred more!

I never met a Beanie Baby wasn't my friend.
And all my little Beanie friends love to pretend
That they're really animals, and that's why I'll spend
My money on a hundred more!

My Beanies live together with me in my house.
In my closet, in my drawers...they're quiet as a mouse.
That's why my mommy lets them sleep in my bed.
In fact, Chocolate the Moose...sleeps right on my head!

Beanie Babies go with me wherever I go.
To school, to the supermarket, out to a show.
To restaurants, and to my aunts, I love them so.
That's why I give them lots of hugs.

I never met a Beanie Baby I didn't like.
All my other toys can go take a hike.
I never met a Beanie Baby I didn't like.
I hope they make a million more!

Beanie Baby

Kid Beanie™

Name	Cost $	Name	Cost $	Name	Cost $
❏ Ally		❏ Derby-Fine		❏ Legs	
❏ Baldy		❏ Derby-Coarse		❏ Libearty	
❏ Batty		❏ Derby-Spot		❏ Lizzy-Tie-Dyed	
❏ Bernie		❏ Digger-Orange		❏ Lizzy-Blue	
❏ Bessie		❏ Digger-Red		❏ Lucky-7	
❏ Blackie		❏ Doby		❏ Lucky-11	
❏ Blizzard		❏ Doodle		❏ Lucky-21	
❏ Bones		❏ Dotty		❏ Magic	
❏ Bongo-Dk Tail		❏ Ears		❏ Manny	
❏ Bongo-Lt Tail		❏ Echo		❏ Maple	
❏ Britannia (1/98)		❏ Flash		❏ Mel	
❏ Bronty		❏ Fleece		Notes	
❏ Brownie		❏ Flip			
❏ Bruno (1/98)		❏ Floppity			
❏ Bubbles		❏ Flutter			
❏ Bucky		❏ Freckles			
❏ Bumble		❏ Garcia			
❏ Caw		❏ Gobbles			
❏ Chilly		❏ Goldie		Mystic	
❏ Chip		❏ Gracie		❏ Fine Yarn	
❏ Chocolate		❏ Grunt		❏ Tan Horn	
❏ Chops		❏ Happy-Grey		❏ Striped Horn	
❏ Claude		❏ Happy-Lav		❏ Nana (Bongo)	
❏ Congo		❏ Hippity		❏ Nanook	
❏ Coral		❏ Hissy (1/98)		❏ Nip-Large	
❏ Crunch		❏ Hoot		❏ Nip-All Gold	
❏ Cubbie		❏ Hoppity		❏ Nip-White Paws	
❏ Curly		❏ Humphrey		❏ Nuts	
❏ Daisy		❏ Iggy (1/98)		❏ Patti-Maroon	
Notes		❏ Inch-Felt		❏ Patti-Purple	
		❏ Inch-Wool		❏ Peace	
		❏ Inky-Tan		Peanut	
		❏ Inky-Pink		❏ Royal Blue	
		❏ Jolly		❏ Light Blue	
		❏ Kiwi		❏ Peking	
		❏ Lefty		❏ Pinchers	

 212

Checklist

How many of the 182 Beanie Babies listed below do you have in your collection?

BLACK = Current   **RED = Retired**

Name	Cost $	Name	Cost $	Name	Cost $
❑ Pinky		❑ Sparky		❑ Violet	
❑ Pouch		❑ Speedy		❑ Violet (Ty Reps)	
❑ Pounce (1/98)		❑ Spike		❑ Trap	
❑ Prance (1/98)		❑ Spinner		❑ Tuffy	
❑ Pride		❑ Splash		❑ Tusk	
❑ Princess		❑ Spooky		❑ Twigs	
❑ Puffer (1/98)		❑ Spot-No Spot		❑ Valentino	
❑ Pugsley		❑ Spot-w/Spot		❑ Velvet	
❑ Punchers		❑ Spunky (1/98)		❑ Waddle	
❑ Quacker-No Wings		❑ Squealer		❑ Waves	
❑ Quackers-Wings		❑ Steg		❑ Web	
❑ Radar		❑ Sting		❑ Weenie	
❑ Rainbow (1/98)		❑ Stinky		❑ Wrinkles	
❑ Rex		❑ Stretch (1/98)		❑ Ziggy	
❑ Righty		❑ Stripes-Dark		❑ Zip-Large	
❑ Ringo		❑ Stripes-Fuzzy		❑ Zip-All Black	
❑ Roary		❑ Stripes-Light		❑ Zip-White Paws	
❑ Rover		❑ Strut		**Teenie Beanies**	
❑ Scoop		❑ Tabasco		❑ Chocolate	
❑ Scottie		❑ Tank-7 Plates		❑ Chops	
❑ Seamore		❑ Tank-9 Plates		❑ Goldie	
❑ Seaweed		❑ Tank-9 Plts (sm)		❑ Lizz	
❑ Slither		❑ 1997 Teddy		❑ Patti	
Notes		**Teddy (Old Face)**		❑ Pinky	
		❑ Brown		❑ Quacks	
		❑ Cranberry		❑ Seamore	
		❑ Jade		❑ Snort	
		❑ Magenta		❑ Speedy	
		❑ Teal		**Notes**	
		❑ Violet			
❑ Sly-Brown Belly		**Teddy (New Face)**			
❑ Sly-White Belly		❑ Brown			
❑ Smoochy (1/98)		❑ Cranberry			
❑ Snip		❑ Jade			
❑ Snort		❑ Magenta			
❑ Snowball		❑ Teal			

The Answer Page

Professor Beanie

Professor Beanie's Quiz

1. Lefty and Righty

2. Bessie, Daisy, Grunt, Humphrey, Peanut, Righty, Snort, Squealer, Tabasco, Trap

3. In 1992 and 1993, some of Ty's "collectible" bears (such as Fraser) were incorrectly identified (on genuine tags) as being part of "The Beanie Baby Collection." These bears have jointed arms and legs and *some* beans.

4. Blizzard, Flip, Mystic, Nanook, Prance, Snip

5. Baldy, Blackie, Blizzard, Bumble, Caw, Congo, Daisy, Doby, Peking, Puffer, Radar, Scottie, Spinner, Splash, Stinky, Stripes, Velvet, Waddle, Waves, Web, Ziggy, Zip

6. Bubbles, Coral, Crunch, Echo, Flash, Flutter, Goldie, Hissy, Inch, Jolly, Manny, Pinchers, Radar, Slither, Snowball, Splash, Spooky, Sting, Waves

7. Orange.

8. Ears.

9. Valentino, of course.

10. Crunch.

11. The authors' Bongo and Congo both weigh the same, 5 ounces apiece.

12. This time it's Bongo!

Who Am Eye?

1. Digger
2. Curly
3. Congo
4. Bones
5. Bessie
6. Bernie
7. Libearty
8. Inky
9. Patti
10. Spike
11. Spooky
12. Trap

Hidden Beanies

1. Bumble
2. Digger
3. Garcia
4. Goldie
5. Hoot
6. Inky
7. Nuts
8. Quackers
9. Righty
10. Speedy
11. Spooky
12. Twigs

Superior Quality Mousse

"I gave 'em name tags with poems, and now they're selling like Beanie Babies!!"